# SPEAKING

*Of*

## $\mathcal{S}$uccess

INSIGHT PUBLISHING
SEVIERVILLE, TENNESSEE

# SPEAKING
## *Of*
# *Success*

Published by Insight Publishing Company
P.O. Box 4189
Sevierville, Tennessee 37864

10 9 8 7 6 5 4 3 2


*Printed in the United States of America*


ISBN: 978-1-60013-111-5

# Table of Contents

# A Message from the Publisher

When we decided to do a series of books on success, we searched long and hard to find just the right combination of authors who were not only a success in business but were successful in their personal life as well.

The authors we found had personal stories to tell that revealed their inner values—values that contributed to the achievements they have made and the positive influence they have on others. These authors are people whom others revere as persons of integrity. They are winners.

Everyone wants to be a winner. I have never met anyone who wants to be a loser. And I'm sure you haven't either. That's why we found some of the best motivational/inspirational speakers and authors in the country to contribute to this series. Some of these men and women are household names. Others are rising stars. All of them have achieved the kind of success all of us want—the kind that sparks enthusiasm in others and leaves an indelible, positive impression.

The road to success is one of hard work and persistence. *Speaking of Success* can help you unlock your potential and inspire you to realize the many possibilities awaiting you as you learn how to remove any mental blocks you might have to the success you deserve.

If you're already well on your way down the success highway, the stories and experiences of these authors will encourage you, inform you, and I guarantee that you will learn something.

It is with great pride that we Insight Publishing present this series, *Speaking of Success*. We think you will discover that you will find something new each time you read through these books.

The chapters in this series are real page-turners, so get ready to be inspired. Get ready to be delighted. Get ready to learn. And remember, *you* are the author of your own success journey. Others can shine a light on the path but you must do the walking.

Interviews conducted by:
David E. Wright
President, International Speakers Network

# *Chapter 1*

## DEANNE DEMARCO

David Wright (Wright)

Today we're talking with Deanne DeMarco, MA, RCC. She is a business coach and communications master who partners with executives and provides insight on how to motivate employees for productivity, increased morale, and to create a more supportive corporate culture where people like to work.

Deanne has won numerous national and international public speaking and professional awards, including recognition by *Training* magazine's "Top 100." Her multicultural training and communication research extends across twenty-eight countries and fifty-two cultures. She was a conflict mediator during the first Gulf War Crisis.

Deanne is author of four books, numerous workbooks, and she has been published in more than fifty trade and professional journals. She is a member of the National Communication Association, The National Speakers Association, The Worldwide Association of Business Coaches, and is certified as a Corporate Coach Instructor.

Deanne, welcome to *Speaking of Success.*

**Deanne DeMarco (DeMarco)**
Thank you.

**Wright**
As a business coach and corporate trainer, what is one secret of success you could share with our readers?

**DeMarco**
One secret of success is the realization that as we travel down the road of life we sometimes need to rebuild the road on which we are traveling. When you drive your car sometimes you will observe a construction crew digging up the old road. The crew will first dig up the old road, lay a new foundation, and then they will resurface the road.

The same is true in our lives. If you want to find personal or professional success you sometimes have to tear up the old road and lay a new foundation before you resurface. Just as in our lives, a quick-fix patch job just doesn't work.

**Wright**
Will you share with our readers some examples of when you need to "repair the road"?

**DeMarco**
An example is a manager who may want to improve performance with either an employee or a team, improve team synergy, or build stronger employee relationships. On an individual basis, you may want better work-life balance in your life, more fulfillment in your career, or you may want to develop stronger personal relationships. In each of these situations, you may need to evaluate the road of your life and rebuild that road.

**Wright**
How can managers improve employee performance by replacing the road?

**DeMarco**
One way is to develop the skill-set of a coach-manager. In the world of sports, athletes hire personal coaches to fine-tune their skills and break through the boundaries to improve performance and achieve goals. In the business world, managers need solid coaching skills to fine-tune individual and team performance in delivering bot-

tom line results. The manager who is able to coach has the ability to make profound improvement in the performance of employees while keeping them motivated.

Coaching is a results-oriented approach that has a completely different skill-set than training, mentoring, managing, or counseling. There is a fine line that separates the interrelated process of coaching, providing feedback, performance appraisals, and managing. Coaching is a goal-centered approach that involves a more dynamic interaction between the coach and the coachee or in this case, the coach-manager and the employee.

Coaching others is an unnatural process for many managers. As a coach-manager you are more centered on asking powerful questions that will help drive performance solutions and improve personal accountability. This process aids the coachee in achieving the ultimate goal. As managers we tend to utilize more of a "telling" rather than an "asking" approach. An asking or non-directive approach is a new skill for most managers. As a manager, one of the most difficult aspects of the job is that balance between using both directive and non-directive approaches with our employees.

## Wright

In your seminars and workshops you teach managers the skills to be an effective coach-manager. What are some the advantages that benefit corporations in training their managers to also be a coach?

## DeMarco

Numerous studies of Fortune 500 companies have clearly shown that correctly coaching employees improves both productivity and job quality. Additionally, organizations that have paired training and coaching together are experiencing outstanding bottom line profitability. For example, stand-alone training may improve productivity by 22 percent while training coupled with coaching increased productivity by as much as 88 percent. Typically, a company can see bottom line results such as:

- Improved productivity—53 percent
- Improved quality—48 percent
- Improved customer satisfaction—39 percent
- Employee retention—32 percent
- Cost reductions—23 percent

In addition, employees who are coached are reporting a number of additional benefits. For example, they are reporting the following:

- Relationships are improved with their direct reports and their managers—70 percent
- Improved teamwork—67 percent
- Improved job satisfaction—61 percent
- Conflict reduction—52 percent
- Improved organizational commitment—44 percent

I have worked with numerous companies implementing coach training initiatives and these managers have reported to me that their actual numbers are statistically higher than the ones I just mentioned. For example, one Fortune 500 manager informed me that conflict in his department had been reduced by over 75 percent and that the morale and teamwork skyrocketed in his department. He acknowledged that prior to the coaching and training initiative, mediating conflict between two of his work groups consumed a great deal of his time. Immediately after the coaching and training initiative the conflict between these two groups almost completely disappeared. He thought it was remarkable that for the first time members of these two conflicting groups were now working together to achieve company objectives without having a referee or without his intervention. He conveyed that the initiative improved work quality, morale, and the harmony within his department was a welcomed bonus.

It has been impressive what companies are experiencing with this coach-manager model.

**Wright**

You said that the coach is centered on asking powerful questions. Would you explain the skill and perhaps give us some examples?

**DeMarco**

The ability to ask powerful questions is probably one of the most important tools the coach-manager has in his or her toolbox. This form of communication is often referred to as the Socratic approach. Through the use of both open- and close-ended questions the coach-manager can help the coachee or employee determine his or her blocks to success, what resources are needed to break through the barriers, and how to reach specific goals and corporate objectives.

The coach-manager utilizes an asking approach instead of a telling approach. For example, let's say a manager has just delegated a project to an employee who is new to project management. The coach-manager might ask questions such as:

- What are some of the goals of this project?
- What are the necessary subtasks that will need to be completed?
- What are the due dates for each project task?
- What are the milestones?
- What barriers do you see with this project?
- What resources do you need in order to be successful in this project?

By asking a series of open-ended questions, the coach-manager-helps the employee think through the complete project.

All too often the manager assumes that the employee understands what is required or the manager tells the employee a string of facts that the employee may not completely grasp.

I heard one horror story about a manager who delegated a complex project to an inexperienced project manger and then expected the employee, on her own, to figure out the process and the tasks to be completed. When the project was not completed to the manager's satisfaction he blamed the employee for poor work. The manager would have been more effective using a coach-manager style rather than a directive approach.

Let me give another example. A manager may want to ask some questions about project goals. Some powerful questions might include:

- What do you want to achieve?
- What is the ideal outcome?
- How are you going to accomplish this goal?
- What steps are necessary in order to achieve this project goal?

If the manager observed some possible barriers hindering the progress of a project, the coach-manager might ask some questions about hindrances such as:

- What barriers are you experiencing?

- What are your options?
- What is wrong with the way you have been approaching this project so far?
- What could prevent you from achieving the project goal?
- What obstacles do you envision? What do you think should be your steps to overcome them?
- What resources do you need?

By asking powerful questions the manager as coach has the employee think through the problem. This process enables the employee to come up with some of the solutions, move forward with the project, and successfully achieve the goal that he or she seeks.

Wright

Would you share a success secret on how a manager could be more effective as a coach-manager?

DeMarco

The ability to adapt one's communication style to the preferred style of the coachee maximizes our effectiveness. Failure to modify your own personal communication style may often result in conflict-prone personal and professional relationships.

Throughout industry, politics, and sports we have seen successful coaches and leaders who exhibit all sorts of behavioral styles. Although there are many different personalities, communication styles can be narrowed down to four major behavioral approaches. These four styles are grounded in the original research that was conducted two thousand years ago by Hippocrates who is known as the "Father of Medicine." In the late 1920s Dr. William Marston, a Harvard-trained psychologist, continued the research that is widely recognized and accepted today.

Over the years, consultants have given these categories their own names, however, they parallel the original distinctions and research made by Hippocrates and Marston. The four styles defined by Marston are: dominance, influence, steadiness, and conscientiousness.

Employees who exhibit the dominance communication style are direct, opinionated, want the bottom line, seek immediate results and enjoy challenges. Communicators who use this style like to win, are risk-takers, and will work hard to get desired results.

To be effective as a coach-manager, show them the simplest and quickest way to be productive. Be firm, direct, and clearly define the limits of their authority. They like public recognition for creating results that make a difference.

The influence style communicators prefer to interact with people; they are fast-paced, animated, enthusiastic, and like to express their thoughts and feelings. These outgoing employees desire results, however, they are very sociable in their interaction. They are excellent communicators and can literally chat with you at length on just about anything.

An effective coach-manger needs to avoid overwhelming details and should request specific feedback to check on the employee's understanding of how to complete a project. Use public praise and provide opportunities for them to interact with others.

Employees who exhibit the steadiness communication style are very accepting of others and are known as the peacemakers. They like cooperation, harmony, and are very good at calming others. This employee likes security, being part of a team, and stability. These people dislike change and are not risk-takers.

With this communicator, the coach-manager needs to use a step-by-step plan for development. Provide one-on-one, hands-on instruction and regular informal feedback on improvements. These are loyal employees who respond positively to group achievements.

Conscientious communication style employees thrive on details and they demand quality. They like to work under known conditions and prefer to follow written standards and procedures. This employee is neat and orderly; he or she values accuracy and has a perfectionist nature.

When managing this communicator, be specific and detailed. Before a meeting, prepare information to be discussed prior to the conversation. The employee exhibiting this communication style will ask many questions, so allow extra time for your meeting.

A work group that has all four styles can be an effective team. Each style brings different strengths to the team. However, it is important for the coach-manager to set a positive tone by demonstrating mutual respect, trust, and acceptance for each style. If the manager can create the right environment and allow the group to motivate themselves, this team can achieve outstanding results.

Wright

How does the coach-manager deal with an employee who is a poor performer?

## DeMarco

There are several schools of thought on this issue. The old school of management states that you should continually eliminate the bottom 10 percent of the workforce. However, I would like to tell you a true story of a young man by the name of Bobby.

Bobby was born with physical limitations. Doctors were all in agreement that Bobby would never be able to run. However, Bobby had another opinion. Bobby wanted to learn how to run.

In sixth grade Bobby joined the track team. Bobby knew the challenges and that the chance of winning a race was slim, however, he showed up every day for practice and he showed up for every track meet. The coach could have easily cut Bobby from the track meets since he clearly was not physically able to compete with the other boys. Instead, this coach embraced Bobby's goal and encouraged him to keep trying.

I will never forget the day when I witnessed this young man run. Bobby was in tenth grade at the time—a sophomore in high school. It was the last race and the last meet of the school year. The boys were all lined up when the gun went off. The boys quickly took off from the starting gate. The event was one lap around the track.

Well, the runners exploded off the starting line and in no time they reached the quarter mark. Bobby was just barely off the starting line. He was running—well, sort of. Bobby's gait was awkward in appearance and clearly not like that of the other boys.

The pack of runners was at the halfway mark and Bobby was far behind. As Bobby crossed the halfway mark all the other boys had finished the race. Three teammates dashed across the field and walked about fifteen feet behind Bobby in the grassy area inside the track field. I wasn't sure what I was watching or what these boys were up to. They shadowed Bobby all the way to the finish line.

I don't think anyone in the bleachers was prepared for what followed. When Bobby crossed the line these three boys made a mad dash toward him. There was massive commotion on the field with students everywhere. There were cheers and screams coming from the crowd. These boys grabbed Bobby and lifted him high above their heads. There was a massive roar from the students who were on the field and in the stands; they crowded around Bobby as he was carried off the field. The students were all cheering for him. You would have thought that Bobby had won the race instead of coming in dead last. Bobby was treated as a hero that day.

I couldn't understand why the boys carried him off so I asked the coach afterward. He told me that because of Bobby the track team ranked first and was impossible to beat. They had won every single race and every single event they had ever competed in during the whole year. The coach told me that Bobby was not fast and he may not win any races but he was a determined competitor. Bobby's encouragement and persistence challenged everyone. Because of Bobby each team member improved his performance one or two seconds at a time—steadily, persistently, everyone improved.

"As a team," the coach said, "we won every event at every meet." Sometimes the team would take first, second, and third place. He said, "A record like ours is unheard of in high school track. Because of Bobby this has been the best team for this or any high school. Normally, the boys are very competitive with each other, but by his example, Bobby showed us how to be a team and how to help each other. Trust formed within the team and encouraging each other was part of the norm." The coach concluded by saying that it had been an incredible year and he had never experienced anything like it.

I think there is a lesson here in Bobby's story. Bobby did not win and he always came in dead last, but because of his desire to improve the team also improved. In business, the accomplishments of the team are greater than the accomplishments of any one person. In order for a manager to be successful, he or she needs a coach-manager mindset to lead a good team. The coach-manger has a skill-set that is supportive of his or her employees. For many managers that will require eliminating the old mindset of power, control, dominance, and leading by threat. That old style of management went out the door with the traditionalists—those born between 1900 and 1945—and definitely with the Baby Boomers—those born between 1946 and 1964.

This Generation X workforce is independent, resilient, adaptable, and technically literate. This group does not respond to the old management styles that worked well in the past. Successful corporations need a productive and loyal workforce and turnover is costly. If companies want to retain their talent the manager needs to re-evaluate his or her managerial style through a whole new filter.

Bobby switched schools and his new coach worked with Bobby using more progressive techniques. He was very effective with Bobby. By the time Bobby graduated from high school, just two years later, Bobby ran a marathon and finished in second place in his age group.

If managers and companies want to be effective with this new workforce, they need to tear up and discard that old road of management and move forward in more progressive techniques by being a coach-manager.

**Wright**

You mentioned earlier that individuals also could benefit from digging up the road before laying a new foundation and a new road. Would you explain?

**DeMarco**

On an individual basis, people who are unhappy with how their life is going—whether they want more work-life balance, happiness in a career, or stronger personal relationships—need to take a realistic look at the road they are presently traveling.

I coached a woman who worked for years as a marketing broker-buyer for an independent grocery store chain. She was successful but wanted a change. Through the discovery process she determined that she wanted to be a paralegal. This is a tough field to enter. Most paralegals prepare for this profession right out of high school. In order for her to reach this dream she needed to tear up her old road and acquire new skills and the education needed for the foundation of her dream. Her persistence paid off. After graduating from paralegal school she got temporary work at one law firm, which led to additional temporary work at another firm. In just over a year she gained considerable experience and secured a full-time job as a paralegal.

Today she is living in the career of her dreams.

**Wright**

What steps do you think are necessary in order to be successful?

**DeMarco**

I think there are basically six steps that we need to look at in rebuilding our road. You can apply these steps in business as well as in personal life. First, people need to identify their dream or their goal and answer two questions: "What would give my life meaning?" What would make my life take on the radiance of a glow stick?"

Watching a construction crew reminds us that the layering of a new road is a process and not a quick fix. Rebuilding a new road or achieving a dream is completed one step at a time, one layer at a time. Both, however, start with the requirement of identification.

Just as the construction worker needs to know which road to tear up, you need to identify your dream!

Second, it is important to visualize what the results are going to look like. This involves clarifying your dream or goal with details. It does not matter how many people believe in your dream or goal, it only takes one person—you—to believe.

If we look at Bobby's story, no one believed that Bobby would be able to run. His parents, doctors, and teachers all agreed that Bobby would never be able to run like a normal child. Yet Bobby believed that he was going to learn how to run.

When clarifying your dream, answer the following two questions: First, what will your dream or goal allow you to do better or more of? Second, how would you describe success? When answering these two questions it is important not to ask friends or family for their thoughts. Often the well-meaning intentions of others don't parallel the desires of our hearts.

The third step is to be committed to rebuilding your road. This is a critical step. Again, the construction crew provides us with the answer. What would our roadways look like if construction crews left roads unfinished? I don't think we would be able to drive anywhere because we would have all these unfinished roads everywhere. The same is true with our own personal success road. We need to commit to the dream; we need to commit to rebuilding our road.

In my coaching practice I have heard many excuses: I'm too old, I'm too young, I'm not clever enough, etc. Yes, it is risky to start down a new path, and to start rebuilding takes courage and a willingness to get off the safe sofa of life and move forward. I truly believe that we can have a more fulfilling life, career, and the relationships of our dreams if we are willing to get involved and be committed to the desires of our hearts and minds.

I once read that success is not measured in dollars but by the quality and quantity of personal satisfaction that it brings. Look at Bobby's story one more time. Bobby showed up for every practice and every track meet. He did not win any race. However, he showed up every day. Every day he made the choice to keep moving forward.

Like Bobby, the choice is ours to make. We can sabotage ourselves with the attitudes and beliefs of our fears. We can sabotage ourselves by listening to the discouraging words of others. We have a clear choice to make. That choice is to either hold back or to move forward. If success is what you desire, then you must make that step of commitment every single day.

Step four is one of discovery—discovering what is possible. Your dream will open new doors, new adventures, and you will meet new people. Possibilities will begin to emerge as you begin to live your dream. In Bobby's story Bobby switched schools and a new coach embraced his dream and started to coach Bobby in a new way. Bobby started to run longer distances and his coach helped him to build upper and lower body strength so that he could start running 5K and 10K races. The coach helped Bobby see new possibilities, which led to his marathon victory. The same is true for our dreams. We need to look for those possibilities that come knocking at our door and look for the opportunities our dream might offer us.

The fifth step is to design a blueprint for success. In step two we looked at where we wanted to go. In this step we need to determine how we are going to get there. What resources are we going to need? What barriers do we need to overcome? Sometimes it is rather painful to develop this to-do list, and the action steps needed to accomplish the tasks.

The last step—step six—is persistence. Every day of every week we need to work toward our dream. In my upcoming book, *Stop Spinning, Start Winning: Strategies for achieving personal and professional success*, I discuss how one needs to do a minimum of two activities every day that will bring value to our dreams. I call it making WOW deposits. WOW stands for "Within One Week." If a person can do at least two activities every day toward his or her dream, then within a week that WOW deposit slip will have at least fourteen line items on it. With every WOW deposit we get closer to realizing our dream and achieving the desires of our hearts.

I think that if we are going to rebuild our road we need to put energy into our dream every day of every week. Bobby never stopped. He showed up for practice. He showed up for every meet. By the time he graduated high school he ran and finished a marathon. I think that in order for us to find success we need to follow that same model. Bobby's story is a powerful metaphor to communicate some important lessons like the power of perseverance and daring to dream big!

**Wright**

What do you think prevents people from becoming successful or realizing their dream?

**DeMarco**

I think the answer to that lies in conquering our fear and developing a courageous attitude. Without the courage to actively pursue our dreams and goals, our dreams can pass us by like clouds carried off by the wind. I think it takes courage to try something new. No dream is realized without persistence and hard work.

According to Webster's Dictionary, courage is that "quality or state of mind or spirit enabling one to face danger or hardship with confidence or resolution." Unfortunately, I think friends and neighbors and family members are great at telling us what we can't do and what we can't accomplish. These well meaning friends are often negative because being negative is easy. If you want to be successful, don't listen to the negative talk of others who try to prevent you from moving forward.

I think my son, Bobby, teaches us the lesson of courage. I will never forget the day he came home telling me he wanted to join the track team. He announced, "Mom, Mom, guess what I found out! I found out I can join the track team. They can't kick me off as long as I show up for every practice and every meet. I don't have to win. I just have to show up!" You know, it took a lot of courage for that young sixth grader. He could barely walk and yet he wanted to join the track team.

How many people have dreams and then fears kick in and they become unwilling to try? I think that to move forward you must show up. Bobby didn't allow anything to get in his way. Bobby showed courage when he joined that track team knowing that he would not win any races. It was clear that Bobby did not have the talent or basic skills to participate on a track team and it took courage to keep showing up day after day, year after year. It would have been easy for him to listen to his peers—"You will never win; you can't run; you can barely walk; you won't be able to contribute anything to the team; you will be the laughing stock of the school; everyone will think you are a fool; people will call you retard." Bobby had the courage to move forward toward his dream even through the cruel and negative comments of his peers.

Moving forward toward your dream requires you to show up every single day of every single year.

**Wright**

What a great conversation. I have learned a lot here today and I am sure that our readers have. I really appreciate your taking all this time with me to answer all these questions. It has really been informative.

**DeMarco**

Thank you. This has been enjoyable.

**Wright**

Today we have been talking with Deanne DeMarco. She is a business coach and communication master. She works with high-level executives and provides insight on how to motivate employees for productivity, increased morale, and to create a more supportive corporate culture where people like to work.

Deanne, thank you so much for being with us today on *Speaking of Success*.

# About the Author

According to a January 2006 article in *Fortune 500* magazine, Generation X workers—those born between 1964 and 1977—require a different management approach than previous generations. Bringing out the best in others, inspiring loyalty, and increasing job satisfaction among members of this elusive group has been the hallmark of Deanne DeMarco's career. Deanne employs a set of strategies aligned with her GenXer Factor™ Management Model to inspire more productivity, passion, and enthusiasm with the younger, Gen-X workforce. This proven approach helps corporations of all sizes create an enthusiastic corporate culture where people achieve more and love to work.

Deanne's unique style and penchant for results has been most affected by her son Bobby's amazing story. "Six months after we brought our son home from the hospital, we started planning for his funeral. Medical tests led doctors to believe that he wouldn't live beyond his first birthday. And, if by some miracle he did survive, he would never walk."

With Deanne's encouragement, Bobby believed he could learn to run and eventually achieved his dream. It was Bobby's example that taught Deanne some of the most powerful lessons that fuel her work with corporations and individuals today.

Deanne's successful training programs are nationally recognized by *Training Magazine's* Top 100. An author, speaker, corporate trainer, and coach, Deanne has written four books, numerous workbooks, and her articles have been published in more than fifty trade and professional journals. Her multicultural training and research extends across twenty-eight countries and fifty-two cultures, including a stint as a conflict mediator during the first Gulf War Crisis.

**Deanne DeMarco, MA, RCC**
Breaking-Boundaries International, Inc.
3013 South Wolf Road, #730
Westchester, Illinois 60154
Phone: 866.91.COACH
E-mail: info@Breaking-Boundaries.com
www.Breaking-Boundaries.com
www.DeanneDeMarco.com

# *Chapter 2*

## DR. KEN BLANCHARD

THE INTERVIEW

### David E. Wright (Wright)

Few people have created a positive impact on the day-to-day management of people and companies more than Dr. Kenneth Blanchard, who is known around the world simply as Ken, a prominent, gregarious, sought-after author, speaker, and business consultant. Ken is universally characterized by friends, colleagues, and clients as one of the most insightful, powerful, and compassionate men in business today. Ken's impact as a writer is far-reaching. His phenomenal bestselling book, *The One Minute Manager®*, co-authored with Spencer Johnson, has sold more than thirteen million copies worldwide and has been translated into more than twenty-five languages. Ken is Chairman and Chief Spiritual Officer of the Ken Blanchard Companies. The organization's focus is to energize organizations around the world with customized training in bottom line business strategies based on the simple, yet powerful principles inspired by Ken's bestselling books.

Dr. Blanchard, welcome to *Speaking of Success!*

### Dr. Ken Blanchard (Blanchard)

Well, it's nice to talk to you, David. It's good to be here.

### Wright

I must tell you that preparing for your interview took quite a bit more time than usual. The scope of your life's work and your business, the Ken Blanchard Companies, would make for a dozen fascinating interviews. Before we dive into the specifics of some of your projects and strategies, will you give our readers a brief synopsis of your life—how you came to be the Ken Blanchard we all know and respect?

### Blanchard

Well, I'll tell you, David, I think life is what you do when you are planning on doing something else. I think that was John Lennon's line. I never intended to do what I have been doing. In fact, all my professors in college told me that I couldn't write. I wanted to do college work, which I did, and they said, "You had better be an administrator." So I decided I was going to be a Dean of Students. I got provisionally accepted into my master's degree program and then provisionally accepted at Cornell, because I never could take any of those standardized tests.

I took the college boards four times and finally got 502 in English. I don't have a test-taking mind. I ended up in a university in Athens, Ohio, in 1966 as an Administrative Assistant to the Dean of the Business School. When I got there he said, "Ken, I want you to teach a course. I want all my deans to teach." I had never thought about teaching because they said I couldn't write, and teachers had to publish. He put me in the manager's department.

I've taken enough bad courses in my day and I wasn't going to teach one. I really prepared and had a wonderful time with the students. I was chosen as one of the top ten teachers on the campus coming out of the chute!

I just had a marvelous time. A colleague by the name of Paul Hersey was chairman of the management department. He wasn't very friendly to me initially because the Dean had led me into his department, but I heard he was a great teacher. He taught organizational behavior and leadership. So I said, "Can I sit in on your course next semester?"

"Nobody audits my courses," he said. "If you want to take it for credit, you're welcome."

I couldn't believe it. I had a doctoral degree and he wanted me to take his course for credit, so I signed up.

The registrar didn't know what to do with me because I already had a doctorate, but I wrote the papers and took the course, and it was great.

In June 1967, Hersey came into my office and said, "Ken, I've been teaching in this field for ten years. I think I'm better than anybody, but I can't write. I'm a nervous wreck, and I'd love to write a textbook with somebody. Would you write one with me?"

I said, "We ought to be a great team. You can't write and I'm not supposed to be able to, so let's do it!"

Thus began this great career of writing and teaching. We wrote a textbook called *Management of Organizational Behavior: Utilizing Human Resources*. It came out in its eighth edition October 3, 2000 and the nineth edition will be out June 15, 2007. It has sold more than any other textbook in that area over the years. It's been over forty years since that book came out.

I quit my administrative job, became a professor, and ended up working my way up the ranks. I got a sabbatical leave and went to California for one year twenty-five years ago. I ended up meeting Spencer Johnson at a cocktail party. He wrote children's books—a wonderful series called *Value Tales for Kids including.* He also wrote *The Value of Courage: The Story of Jackie Robinson and The Value of Believing In Yourself: The Story Louis Pasteur.*

My wife, Margie, met him first and said, "You guys ought to write a children's book for managers because they won't read anything else." That was my introduction to Spencer. So, *The One Minute Manager* was really a kid's book for big people. That is a long way from saying that my career was well planned.

### Wright

Ken, what and/or who were your early influences in the areas of business, leadership and success? In other words, who shaped you in your early years?

### Blanchard

My father had a great impact on me. He was retired as an admiral in the Navy and had a wonderful philosophy. I remember when I was elected as president of the seventh grade, and I came home all pumped up. My father said, "Son, it's great that you're the president of the seventh grade, but now that you have that leadership position, don't ever use it." He said, "Great leaders are followed because people respect them and like them, not because they have power." That was a wonderful lesson for me early on. He was just a great model for me. I got a lot from him.

Then I had this wonderful opportunity in the mid 1980s to write a book with Norman Vincent Peale. He wrote *The Power of Positive Thinking*. I met him when he was eighty-six years old and we were asked to write a book on ethics together, *The Power of Ethical Management: Integrity Pays, You Don't Have to Cheat to Win*. It didn't matter what we were writing together, I learned so much from him, and he just built from the positive things I learned from my mother.

My mother said that when I was born I laughed before I cried, I danced before I walked, and I smiled before I frowned. So that, as well as Norman Vincent Peale, really impacted me as I focused on what I could do to train leaders. How do you make them positive? How do you make them realize that it's not about them, it's about who they are serving. It's not about their position, it's about what they can do to help other people win.

So, I'd say my mother and father, then Norman Vincent Peale, all had a tremendous impact on me.

### Wright

I can imagine. I read a summary of your undergraduate and graduate degrees. I assumed you studied business administration, marketing management, and related courses. Instead, at Cornell you studied government and philosophy. You received your master's from Colgate in sociology and counseling and your PhD from Cornell in educational administration and leadership. Why did you choose this course of study? How has it affected your writing and consulting?

### Blanchard

Well, again, it wasn't really well planned out. I originally went to Colgate to get a master's degree in education because I was going to be a Dean of Students over men. I had been a government major, and I was a government major because it was the best department at Cornell in the Liberal Arts School. It was exciting. We would study what the people were doing at the league governments. And then, the Philosophy Department was great. I just loved the philosophical arguments. I wasn't a great student in terms of getting grades, but I'm a total learner. I would sit there and listen, and I would really soak it in.

When I went over to Colgate and got in these education courses, they were awful. They were boring. The second week, I was sitting at the bar at the Colgate Inn saying, "I can't believe I've been here two years for this." It's just the way the Lord works—sitting next to me in the bar was a young sociology professor who had just gotten his PhD at Illinois. He was staying at the Inn. I was moaning and groaning about what I was doing, and he said, "Why don't you come and major with me in sociology? It's really exciting."

"I can do that?" I asked.

He said, "Yes."

I knew they would probably let me do whatever I wanted the first week. Suddenly, I switched out of education and went with Warren Ramshaw. He had a tremendous impact on me. He retired some years ago as the leading professor at Colgate in the Arts and Sciences, and got me interested in leadership and organizations. That's why I got a master's in sociology.

The reason I went into educational administration and leadership? It was a doctoral program I could get into because I knew the guy heading up the program. He said, "The greatest thing about Cornell is that you will be in a School of Education. It's not very big, so you don't have to take many education courses, and you can take stuff all over the place."

There was a marvelous man by the name of Don McCarty, who eventually became the Dean of the School of Education, Wisconsin. He had an impact on my life; but I was always just searching around. My mission statement is: to be a loving teacher and example of simple truths that help myself and others to awaken the presence of God in our lives. The reason I mention "God" is that I believe the biggest addiction in the world is the human ego; but I'm really into simple truth. I used to tell people I was trying to get the B.S. out of the behavioral sciences.

**Wright**

I can't help but think, when you mentioned your father, that he just bottomed lined it for you about leadership.

**Blanchard**

Yes.

**Wright**

A man named Paul Myers, in Texas, years and years ago when I went to a conference down there, said, "David, if you think you're a leader and you look around, and no one is following you, you're just out for a walk."

**Blanchard**

Well, you'd get a kick; I'm just reaching over to pick up a picture of Paul Myers on my desk. He's a good friend, and he's a part of our Center for FaithWalk Leadership where we're trying to challenge and equip people to lead like Jesus. It's non-profit. I tell people I'm not an evangelist because we've got enough trouble with the Christians we have. We don't need any more new ones. But, this is a picture of Paul on top of a mountain. Then there's another picture below that of him under the sea with stingrays. It says, "Attitude is everything. Whether you're on the top of the mountain or the bottom of the sea, true happiness is achieved by accepting God's promises, and by having a biblically positive frame of mind. Your attitude is everything." Isn't that something?

**Wright**

He's a fine, fine man. He helped me tremendously. In keeping with the theme of our book, *Speaking of Success,* I wanted to get a sense from you about your own success journey. Many people know you best from *The One Minute Manager* books you coauthored with Spencer Johnson. Would you consider these books as a high water mark for you, or have you defined success for yourself in different terms?

**Blanchard**

Well, you know, *The One Minute Manager* was an absurdly successful book, so quickly that I found I couldn't take credit for it. That was when I really got on my own spiritual journey and started to try to find out what the real meaning of life and success was.

That's been a wonderful journey for me because I think, David, the problem with most people is they think their self-worth is a function of their performance plus the opinion of others. The minute you think that is what your self-worth is, every day your self-worth is up for grabs because your performance is going to fluctuate on a day-to-day basis. People are fickle. Their opinions are going to go up and down. You need to ground your self-worth in the unconditional love that

God has ready for us, and that really grew out of the unbelievable success of *The One Minute Manager.*

When I started to realize where all that came from, that's how I got involved in this ministry that I mentioned. Paul Myers is a part of it. As I started to read the Bible, I realized that everything I've ever written about, or taught, Jesus did. You know, He did it with the twelve incompetent guys He "hired." The only guy with much education was Judas, and he was His only turnover problem.

**Wright**
    Right.

**Blanchard**
    It was a really interesting thing. What I see in people is not only do they think their self-worth is a function of their performance plus the opinion of others, but they measure their success on the amount of accumulation of wealth, on recognition, power, and status. I think those are nice success items. There's nothing wrong with those, as long as you don't define your life by that.

What I think you need to focus on rather than success is what Bob Buford, in his book *Halftime,* calls significance—moving from success to significance. I think the opposite of accumulation of wealth is generosity.

I wrote a book called *The Generosity Factor* with Truett Cathy, who is the founder of Chick-fil-A. He is one of the most generous men I've ever met in my life. I thought we needed to have a model of generosity. It's not only your treasure, but it's your time and talent. Truett and I added *touch* as a fourth one.

The opposite of recognition is service. I think you become an adult when you realize you're here to serve rather than to be served.

Finally, the opposite of power and status is loving relationships. Take Mother Teresa as an example; she couldn't have cared less about recognition, power, and status because she was focused on generosity, service, and loving relationships; but she got all of that earthly stuff. If you focus on the earthly, such as money, recognition, and power, you're never going to get to significance. But if you focus on significance, you'll be amazed at how much success can come your way.

**Wright**

I spoke with Truett Cathy recently and was impressed by what a down-to-earth, good man he seems to be. When you start talking about him closing on Sunday, all of my friends—when they found out I had talked to him—said, "Boy, he must be a great Christian man, but he's rich and all this." I told them, "Well, to put his faith into perspective, by closing on Sunday it cost him $500 million a year."

He lives his faith, doesn't he?

**Blanchard**

Absolutely, but he still outsells everybody else.

**Wright**

That's right.

**Blanchard**

According to their January 25, 2007, press release, Chick-fil-A is currently the nation's second-largest quick-service chicken restaurant chain in sales. Its business performance marks the thirty-ninth consecutive year the chain has enjoyed a system-wide sales gain—a streak the company has sustained since opening its first chain restaurant in 1967.

**Wright**

The simplest market scheme, I told him, tripped me up. I walked by his first Chick-fil-A I had ever seen, and some girl came out with chicken stuck on toothpicks and handed me one; I just grabbed it and ate it, it's history from there on.

**Blanchard**

Yes, I think so. It's really special. It is so important that people understand generosity, service, and loving relationships because too many people are running around like a bunch of peacocks. You even see pastors who measure their success by how many in are in their congregation; authors by how many books they have sold; businesspeople by what their profit margin is—how good sales are. The reality is that's all well and good, but I think what you need to focus on is the other. I think if business did that more and we got Wall Street off our backs with all the short-term evaluation, we'd be a lot better off.

**Wright**

Absolutely. There seems to be a clear theme that winds through many of your books that have to do with success in business and organizations—how people are treated by management and how they feel about their value to a company. Is this an accurate observation? If so, can you elaborate on it?

**Blanchard**

Yes, it's a very accurate observation. See, I think the profit is the applause you get for taking care of your customers and creating a motivating environment for your people. Very often people think that business is only about the bottom line. But no, that happens to be the result of creating raving fan customers, which I've described with Sheldon Bowles in our book, *Raving Fans*. Customers want to brag about you, if you create an environment where people can be gung-ho and committed. You've got to take care of your customers and your people, and then your cash register is going to go ka-ching, and you can make some big bucks.

**Wright**

I noticed that your professional title with the Ken Blanchard Companies is somewhat unique—Chairman and Chief Spiritual Officer. What does your title mean to you personally and to your company? How does it affect the books you choose to write?

**Blanchard**

I remember having lunch with Max DuPree one time, the legendary Chairman of Herman Miller, who wrote a wonderful book called *Leadership Is An Art*. "What's your job?" I asked him.

He said, "I basically work in the vision area."

"Well, what do you do?" I asked.

"I'm like a third grade teacher," he replied. "I say our vision and values over, and over, and over again until people get it right, right, right."

I decided from that, I was going to become the Chief Spiritual Officer, which means I would be working in the vision, values, and energy part of our business. I ended up leaving a morning message every day for everybody in our company. We have twenty-eight international offices around the world. I leave a voice mail every morning, and I do three things on that as Chief Spiritual Officer: One, people tell me who we need to pray for. Two, people tell me who we need to praise—

our unsung heroes and people like that. And then three, I leave an inspirational morning message. I really am the cheerleader—the Energizer Bunny—in our company. I'm the reminder of why we're here and what we're trying to do.

We think that our business in the Ken Blanchard Companies is to help people lead at a higher level, and to help individuals and organizations. Our mission statement is to unleash the power and potential of people and organizations for the common good. So if we are going to do that, we've really got to believe in that.

I'm working on getting more Chief Spiritual Officers around the country. I think it's a great title and we should get more of them.

**Wright**

So those people for whom you pray, where do you get the names?

**Blanchard**

The people in the company tell me who needs help, whether it's a spouse who is sick, or kids who are sick, or they are worried about something. We've got over five years of data about the power of prayer, which is pretty important.

One morning, my inspirational message was about my wife and five members of our company who walked sixty miles one weekend—twenty miles a day for three days—to raise money for breast cancer research.

It was amazing. I went down and waved them all in as they came. They had a ceremony, and they had raised 7.6 million dollars. There were over three thousand people walking, and a lot of the walkers were dressed in pink; they were cancer victors—people who had overcome it. There were even men walking with pictures of their wives who had died from breast cancer. I thought it was incredible.

There wasn't one mention about it in the major San Diego papers. I said, "Isn't that just something." We have to be an island of positive influence because all you see in the paper today is about Michael Jackson and Scott Peterson and Kobe Bryant—celebrities and their bad behavior—and here you get all these thousands of people out there walking and trying to make a difference, and nobody thinks it's news.

So every morning I pump people up about what life's about, about what's going on. That's what my Chief Spiritual Officer job is about.

**Wright**

I had the pleasure of reading one of your releases, *The Leadership Pill*.

**Blanchard**

Yes.

**Wright**

I must admit that my first thought was how short the book was. I wondered if I was going to get my money's worth, which by the way, I most certainly did. Many of your books are brief and based on a fictitious story. Most business books in the market today are hundreds of pages in length and are read almost like a textbook.

Will you talk a little bit about why you write these short books, and about the premise of *The Leadership Pill*?

**Blanchard**

I really developed my relationship with Spencer Johnson when we wrote *The One Minute Manager*. As you know, he wrote, *Who Moved My Cheese*, which was a phenomenal success. He wrote children's books, and is quite a storyteller.

Jesus taught by parables, which were short stories.

My favorite books are, *Jonathan Livingston Seagull* and *The Little Prince*.

Og Mandino, author of seventeen books, was the greatest of them all.

I started writing parables because people can get into the story and learn the contents of the story, and they don't bring their judgmental hats into reading. You write a regular book and they'll say, "Well, where did you get the research?" They get into that judgmental side. Our books get them emotionally involved and they learn.

*The Leadership Pill* is a fun story about a pharmaceutical company who thinks that they have discovered the secret to leadership, and they can put the ingredients in a pill. When they announce it, the country goes crazy because everybody knows we need more effective leaders. When they release it, it outsells Viagra. The founders of the company start selling off stock and they call them Pillionaires. But along comes this guy who calls himself "the effective manager," and he challenges them to a no-pill challenge. If they identify two non-performing groups, he'll take on one and let somebody on the pill take another one, and he guarantees he will out-perform that person by the end of the year. They agree, but of course they give him a drug test every week to make sure he's not sneaking pills on the side.

I wrote the book with Marc Muchnick, who is a young guy in his early thirties. We did a major study of what this interesting "Y" generation, the young people of today, want from leaders, and this is a secret blend that this effective manager uses. When you think about it, David, it is really powerful on terms of what people want from a leader.

Number one, they want integrity. A lot of people have talked about that in the past, but these young people will walk if they see people say one thing and do another. A lot of us walk to the bathroom and out into the halls to talk about it. But these people will quit. They don't want somebody to say something and not do it.

The second thing they want is a partnership relationship. They hate superior/subordinate. I mean, what awful terms those are. You know, the "head" of the department and the hired "hands"—you don't even give them a head. "What do you do? I'm in supervision. I see things a lot clearer than these stupid idiots." They want to be treated as partners; if they can get a financial partnership, great. If they can't, they really want a minimum of psychological partnership where they can bring their brains to work and make decisions.

Then finally, they want affirmation. They not only want to be caught doing things right, but they want to be affirmed for who they are. They want to be known as a person, not as a number.

So those are the three ingredients that this effective manager uses. They are wonderful values when you think about them.

Rank-order values for any organization is number one, integrity. In our company we call it ethics. It is our number one value. The number two value is partnership. In our company we call it relationships. Number three is affirmation—being affirmed as a human being. I think that ties into relationships, too. They are wonderful values that can drive behavior in a great way.

### Wright

I believe most people in today's business culture would agree that success in business has everything to do with successful leadership. In *The Leadership Pill*, you present a simple but profound premise, that leadership is not something you do to people, it's something you do *with* them. At face value, that seems incredibly obvious. But you must have found in your research and observations that leaders in today's culture do not get this. Would you speak to that issue?

**Blanchard**

Yes. I think what often happens in this is the human ego. There are too many leaders out there who are self-serving. They're not leaders who have service in mind. They think the sheep are there for the benefit of the shepherd. All the power, money, fame, and recognition moves up the hierarchy; they forget that the real action in business is not up the hierarchy; it's in the one-to-one, moment-to-moment interactions that your front line people have with your customers. It's how the phone is answered. It's how problems are dealt with and those kinds of things. If you don't think that you're doing leadership *with* them—rather, you're doing it to them—after a while they won't take care of your customers.

I was at a store once (not Nordstrom's, where I normally would go) and I thought of something I had to share with my wife, Margie. I asked the guy behind the counter in Men's Wear, "May I use your phone?"

He said, "No!"

"You're kidding me," I said. "I can always use the phone at Nordstrom's."

"Look, buddy," he said, "they won't let *me* use the phone here. Why should I let you use the phone?"

That is an example of leadership that's done *to* employees not *with* them. People want a partnership. People want to be involved in a way that really makes a difference.

**Wright**

Dr. Blanchard, the time has flown by and there are so many more questions I'd like to ask you. In closing, would you mind sharing with our readers some thoughts on success? If you were mentoring a small group of men and women, and one of their central goals was to become successful, what kind of advice would you give them?

**Blanchard**

Well, I would first of all say, "What are you focused on?" If you are focused on success as being, as I said earlier, accumulation of money, recognition, power, or status, I think you've got the wrong target. What you need to really be focused on is how you can be generous in the use of your time and your talent and your treasure and touch. How can you serve people rather than be served? How can you develop caring, loving relationships with people? My sense is if you will focus on those things, success in the traditional sense will come to you. But if you go out and say, "Man, I'm going to make a fortune, and I'm going to do this," and have that kind of attitude, you might get some of those numbers. I think you become an adult, however, when you realize you are here to give rather than to get. You're here to serve not to be served. I would just say to people, "Life is such a very special occasion. Don't miss it by aiming at a target that bypasses other people, because we're really here to serve each other." So that's what I would share with people.

### Wright

Well, what an enlightening conversation, Dr. Blanchard. I really want you to know how much I appreciate all the time you've taken with me for this interview. I know that our readers will learn from this, and I really appreciate your being with us today.

### Blanchard

Well, thank you so much, David. I really enjoyed my time with you. You've asked some great questions that made me think, and I hope my answers are helpful to other people because as I say, life is a special occasion.

### Wright

Today we have been talking with Dr. Ken Blanchard. He is the author of the phenomenal best selling book, *The One Minute Manager*. The fact that he's the Chief Spiritual Officer of his company should make us all think about how we are leading our companies and leading our families and leading anything, whether it is in church or civic organizations. I know I will.

Thank you so much, Dr. Blanchard, for being with us today on *Speaking of Success*.

### Blanchard

Good to be with you, David.

## About The Author

Few people have created more of a positive impact on the day-to-day management of people and companies than Dr. Kenneth Blanchard, who is known around the world simply as "Ken."

When Ken speaks, he speaks from the heart with warmth and humor. His unique gift is to speak to an audience and communicate with each individual as if they were alone and talking one-on-one. He is a polished storyteller with a knack for making the seemingly complex easy to understand.

Ken has been a guest on a number of national television programs, including *Good Morning America* and *The Today Show*. He has been featured in *Time, People, U.S. News & World Report*, and a host of other popular publications.

He earned his bachelor's degree in government and philosophy from Cornell University, his master's degree in sociology and counseling from Colgate University, and his PhD in educational administration and leadership from Cornell University.

**Dr. Ken Blanchard**
The Ken Blanchard Companies
125 State Place
Escondido, California 92029
Phone: 800.728.6000
Fax: 760.489.8407
www.kenblanchard.com

# Chapter 3

## DUSTIN HILLIS

THE INTERVIEW

**David Wright (Wright)**

Today we're talking with Dustin Hillis. He is an expert on sales fundamentals, and through his teaching he provides people with tools and techniques for improving execution. His foundation was forged from his years of direct sales with The Southwestern Company, a 150-year-old sales training company with over 3,500 salespeople worldwide. Dustin finished number one in his first year with Southwestern, then he eclipsed the all-time company record making a profit of over $100,000 in fourteen weeks. During that time he was also a junior in college. Mr. Hillis is a top sales professional and as a product of Southwestern, he is now a founding partner in the Southwestern Seminars division known as Success Starts Now!™ He is a motivational speaker, professional trainer, and confidence coach.

Dustin, welcome to *Speaking of Success!*

**Dustin Hillis (Hillis)**

Thank you for having me.

**Wright**

What were the three toughest challenges you have ever had to overcome?

**Hillis**

I don't look at a challenge as a problem, but instead as an opportunity to grow in the three main areas of my life: personal, physical, and business. I am thankful for the challenges in my life and the character developed from those challenges.

In my personal life, I would say that the number one challenge was convincing my wife, Kyah, to marry me—that was the best sale I've ever made!

A physical challenge was in high school when I was the state finalist in wrestling. Making the state finals was a big challenge and an exciting goal to achieve. It really helped my confidence in the long run.

Another challenge I have faced is in my business endeavors. I set a goal to break the Southwestern all-time company sales record. You know that turn you sometimes feel in your stomach—those butterflies? That's the feeling I had when I set that goal. I was going into my third year of working with Southwestern and wanted to break the company record! When I set that goal it was refreshing to have something I knew would challenge me that I could put my mind to and work through.

Those were my top three challenges.

**Wright**

As a professional sales trainer, motivational speaker, and confidence coach for Success Starts Now!™, what motivated you to choose the field of professional speaking?

**Hillis**

My speaking and sales training career started at Southwestern. After breaking the company record in my third year, I participated in a lot of the sales training throughout the company, both on a national and global scale. My first big keynote speech was the European Great Recruiter's Seminar in London. Prior to this speaking event, I hadn't thought of training or coaching; I was just focusing on being a top producer. After my first presentation, a new passion built up inside of me. Before I walked out on stage I felt as though I was about to go and play a football game! The company made a CD out of that speech—and then asked me to make the same speech at the Great Recruiter's Seminar in the United States in front of more than 1,000 people.

After those two speaking events, I received a lot of great feedback regarding the techniques for increasing belief levels and doubling production. Students and managers shared success stories that they had after listening to my CD—and hearing that was all I needed. It helped those people reach and achieve their personal goals. Then I decided to give as much help as possible and started booking myself with any sales manager who wanted to have me speak to his or her group.

Southwestern and Success Starts Now!™ asked me to be one of the founding partners and bring the philosophies of The Southwestern Company to the professional sales world. It's something I love; it's exciting talking about selling and helping people reach their goals both personally and professionally!

**Wright**

Southwestern's Success Starts Now!™ sales training division teaches the execution of fundamentals. What does that mean?

**Hillis**

We don't teach tricks. We don't talk about gimmicks that get people to buy product. We focus on techniques and principles that have been proven to work time and time again. Southwestern is a 150-year-old direct sales company. Every year 3,500 college students work out of state going door-to-door to sell educational reference books, software, and CDs to help students save time on homework.

Anyone who has forged his or her success principles in door-to-door selling will hear other sales managers and sales professionals say, "If you can do direct sales and you can sell books door-to-door, you can sell anything."

Execution of the fundamentals is our focus and we provide techniques or tools on how to be successful. The principles that Southwestern teaches are hard work, positive mental attitude, and how to work like a true sales professional by following the cycle of the sale.

Southwestern provides training on how to execute the cycle of the sale, which is something every salesperson does consciously or subconsciously when a sale is made. Sales professionals know the psychology behind why the selling cycle is important. It is designed to save time and increase production by following these seven steps:

1. Prospecting/Pre-Approach
2. Initial Contact
3. Qualifying
4. Presentation
5. Answering Objections
6. Closing
7. Referrals/Follow up

**Wright**

What's the difference between a top producer and an average producer?

**Hillis**

The common thread of all top producers is the combination of habits they form and act out every single day. In the book *The Common Denominator of Success,* Albert Gray relates that, "The common denominator of success—the secret of success of every man who has ever been successful—lies in the fact that he formed the habit of doing things that failures don't like to do." Top producers believe in that, and if you form the right habits you will become a top producer much faster.

All top producers form three common habits regardless of the industry:

1. They focus on being a student of the game. They always want to learn and expand their knowledge base. They are willing to be impacted with that knowledge and internalize it to use it. They never stop learning.

2. Top producers are competitive and always believe that the difference between being an average producer and a top producer is that you have to have a competitive edge. Being competitive is not necessarily a gift or innate, but the key is conditioning yourself to be competitive with everything you do. This doesn't mean only being competitive with others—it can also mean self-competition that will drive you to success.

   At Success Starts Now!™, we talk about techniques for setting goals designed for hitting your Maximum Earning Potential (M.E.P.). We teach about taking incremental steps to hit a large goal; we call this "The Slight Edge." It's defined as doing an activity a little bit more than the competition every single day. This results in a huge difference that will separate you from the competition. For example: A marksman is shooting at a bull's-eye a mile away. If he adjusts his sights one click, it will result in a major change in the direction of the bullet and whether or not it hits the bull's-eye. If the marksman clicks his sight more than one click he could be completely off the target!

3. Top producers are goal oriented. They review their goals daily and have action items to achieve their goals. They are also accountable to those goals. My business partner, and one of our motivational speakers, Gary Michels, has developed what's called "The Ideal Wheel." You set goals through the seven different quadrants of your life and put action items on how to hit your goal. You share your action items with an accountability partner who can help you get there.

The difference between average producers and top producers are these three habits:

1. Be a student of the Game. Be like a sponge and absorb knowledge all the time. No matter what your production level is, you can always do better.

2. Cultivate a competitive edge with yourself and others by using The Slight Edge theory.

3. Set goals daily and focus on action items that help you hit the goal.

That is the Southwestern winning formula.

**Wright**

What are the factors needed to reach Maximum Earning Potential and finish number one?

**Hillis**

The reason people do not reach their true potential is because they subconsciously build barriers that cause self-doubt. They don't believe they can hit high goals. The three most important characteristics for breaking belief barriers are commitment, control, and confidence.

1. Commitment is doing the work—putting in the effort with no excuses! Top producers do not make excuses; they stay committed.

   When I think of commitment I am reminded of a time when I was working in Southwest Missouri in McDonald County. I was selling books door-to-door. While in Missouri, I had over ten flat tires in three months! I had so many flat tires I started timing myself with a stopwatch as if I were on a NASCAR pit crew. So I find myself in the middle of nowhere, on a mile-long driveway (scenery common to that area). The driveway passed through a canopy of trees.

   As I was changing the tire trying to beat my pit crew record time, I noticed my arm looked like my skin was crawling. Upon further inspection I realized I was completely covered in ticks! I don't know about you, but when people ask me what my favorite critter is I don't say ticks. So what did I do? I reacted the same way any other rational human being would—I flipped out! I stripped down buck naked and threw my clothes in a plastic bag so ticks would not get in the car. Then I drove to the nearest gas station. I hopped out, but realized I'd better put my pants back on. So after that embarrassing incident, I ran into the gas station with no shirt and no shoes.

   An older lady looked at me and said "Son, what's wrong with you?" I replied "I've got *ticks!*" So I grabbed a razor and ran to the bathroom. Now as I was looking at myself in the mirror and trying to pick the ticks off, I had a deep sense of doubt. I wanted to quit what I was doing, go home, and use this as a reason why I didn't hit my goal. But, something inside of me said No. I had committed to my sales manager, my friends, parents, and (more importantly) to myself I was not going to quit on a single day, week, or month. So I shaved the ticks off one by one. I went on and finished my day. That day was not my most productive day, but it was my most important because after that experience I knew nothing would stop me from fulfilling my commitments from then on.

2. There are certain things in life that we cannot control, such as death, natural disasters, flat tires, ticks, or even who buys from us. Top producers realize this so they focus

on controlling the controllable factors. Those factors are the number of hours we work, the amount of calls or prospecting we do in a day, and our attitude.

Now you're probably saying "that sounds good, but how am I supposed to do this?" We teach a technique called R.A.F.T. This helps harness emotion from an uncontrollable event and creates a positive outcome. R.A.F.T. is an acronym that stands for:

Realize an event is occurring.

Accept the situation.

Focus on the controllable (hours, calls, and attitude).

Transform the negative emotion into positive momentum.

I came up with this technique when I was working in Fairbanks, Alaska—the only place on earth you will see a sign that says "North Pole, next exit." One day I received a call from my teenage brother.

"Hello."

"Dude, we have to talk . . . it's about Mom and Dad."

My parents had been married for twenty-five years and on that day I found out they were getting a divorce. I felt mad, frustrated, confused, and worst of all, I couldn't find the number for Dr. Phil—my head was out of the ballgame. So I applied the R.A.F.T. technique:

- Realized an event was occurring—by my productivity stopping.
- Accepted the situation—even though I didn't want to.
- Focused on my hours and calls. My attitude was hard to control so I was using positive phrases to keep my Positive Mental Attitude (P.M.A.) right. (More about P.M.A. later.)
- Transformed the negative energy into positive momentum by putting on the blinders and going to work.

In spite of how I felt emotionally, this technique helped me focus professionally. Everyone has moments fraught with personal conflict or hardship, but it doesn't need to be an excuse that hinders you in the workplace. My parents' situation was out of control, but by applying the R.A.F.T. technique, I focused on what I could control. As a result, I made more commission that week than anyone in the history of The Southwestern Company. As a junior in college, in one week I made over $15,000 and had over sixty customers selling books door-to-door!

3. The last factor in breaking belief barriers and becoming number one in your industry is unconditional confidence. Why is unconditional confidence important? People are attracted to it, it evokes trust, and people will be led to take action by unconditional confidence.

**Wright**

What is Unconditional Confidence and how is it defined?

**Hillis**

There are three types of confidence: False, Conditional, and Unconditional.

- False Confidence is saying you can do something, but deep down inside you think there is no way you can actually do the task. It's negative self-talk. A good example is someone who, when with their group of friends talks and acts as though they were superman or superwoman, but when put into an unfamiliar selling situation, they change from superman to super-scared. False confidence comes from F.E.A.R. which is defined by Tony Robbins as False Evidence Appearing Real.

- Conditional Confidence is why this job can be frustrating. The job of sales can be emotional. Why do you think that is? It's because we attach our self-worth to whether or not we make a sale. Many people have made one, two, or three sales in a row and their confidence goes way up. Then they go a day, a week, or a month with no sales and what happens to their confidence? Right! It hits peaks and valleys like a roller coaster. This confidence is conditional on the outcome.

- The last and most important factor that separates all top producers from average producers is *unconditional confidence.*

Top Producers who strive for unconditional confidence have that something special—charisma, or what Austin Powers would call it: "mojo."

Unconditional confidence is based on knowing that you do have skills. The key is that your self-worth is not attached to how much you produce; your self-worth is based on effort.

A good positive affirmation to use when forming unconditional confidence is saying to yourself every day when you look into the mirror:

"I do not expect success all the time, but due to the belief in my own abilities and acquired skills I can be fearless in the moment. In reality, self-worth has nothing to do with the outcome. So when the pressure comes, I cannot hesitate. Knowing sometimes I will do well and sometimes I won't, regardless, I know failure is temporary and success will happen with perseverance."

**Wright**

How did you finish number one out of 3,500 salespeople at the Southwestern Company year after year, and even finish number one your first year?

**Hillis**

People are only as successful as the people with whom they choose to associate. How anyone can become a top producer starts with the mentors and influences surrounding them.

Some good examples are the role models I have chosen to learn from and who helped instill the belief and the drive that it takes to consistently be a top producer.

To start with, my grandfather taught me to never back down. When adversity comes, always stand up for what you believe and walk tall with the presence of someone who knows what he wants. So even if it's your first year of going into a business where a lot of people might be better than you are, if you believe in yourself then you can do anything you set your mind to do.

Then my dad taught me honesty, integrity, and faith. The reason people buy from you is because they like you and trust you. If you are honest and never misleading, they will trust you. Trust is instilled when your customer knows you want to do what's right for the betterment of the group you are working with, and they will like you and trust you in return. I always remember my dad saying, "I don't care *who* is right, I care about *what* is right." Adopting that philosophy engenders respect and trust.

My role models in athletics were wrestling and football coaches. They helped instill in my character a good work ethic and they helped infuse mental toughness within myself. To be the number one top producer in the field of sales you have to be mentally tough. You have to have a competitive edge and you have to have confidence. You have to know that anything is possible as long as you work hard and you are determined. I think I got that from my athletic coaches.

And then finally, what really forged all of this together and refined my techniques was working with The Southwestern Company. They took everything that I had gained from the past and then taught me techniques and systems that focused my energy into something productive.

For parents who have kids in college, or for those who are college age, The Southwestern Company of Nashville, Tennessee, is the best opportunity—not only to make a good amount of money while you're in college and during the summertime—but it's also the best opportunity for future employment and for developing the skills it takes to be a top producer upon entering the career arena of sales. At The Southwestern Company, you will find mentors and coaches to help guide you in the direction of success.

**Wright**

What skills did you develop working with Southwestern?

**Hillis**

The Southwestern Company's philosophy is "We build people, and people build companies." The coaches and trainers at Southwestern helped me develop traits I did not naturally have, such as attention to details. Being detail oriented is not a natural gift for many people, however, when one follows through on a daily detailed plan, a great deal of satisfaction and accomplishment results. People can become successful by doing the little, often mundane things that it takes to be successful. Being detail oriented in sales means two things:

One is focusing on the Cycle of the Sale as previously outlined. By making sure that every customer is qualified, getting objections out on the table, and eliminating procrastination by asking questions such as, "If we were to meet your needs, would this be something we could move forward with today, or should somebody else be involved in the decision-making process?" By asking questions this way, focus is on details and the small steps it takes to make a big difference in increasing personal production—The Slight Edge.

Another example of focusing on details is after meeting sales prospects, make sure to touch base with them six times. Send thank-you cards, make them feel important and special. Doing that will encourage people to like you and trust you—that's why they buy from you.

The second detail on which top producers focus is using positive affirmations and having a Positive Mental Attitude (P.M.A.). The techniques used in conditioning a P.M.A. are using positive affirmations and telling yourself what you are going to do before you do it, and then believing that you can do what you told yourself. Through positive affirmation your belief level is raised and you expect that whatever you're telling yourself over and over is going to happen. For example, if you call your customers and you are having negative thoughts about whether they will buy, then they're probably not going to buy. But if you're telling yourself all day long, "Everyone's getting them; this is going to be great," your reality is probably going to be success with your sales.

Focusing on those two things will be the difference between average producers and top producers.

## Wright

When you broke the 150-year-old Southwestern Company sales record, you made a personal profit of over $100,000 in a matter of fourteen weeks and you did this while you were a junior in college. How did that feel?

## Hillis

As a junior in college, it was great! To be honest, that summer it was more of a relief to just reach my goal and break the company record—I was not even concerned with the amount of money I was making. That's how focused I was on doing what I said I was going to do and hitting my goal. At Southwestern we keep track of production in units. With the goal to sell 20,000 units and after having sold 9,000 units the summer before (which was a really good year), my goal was to double my production. Then when I came out of the summer, and I actually hit the goal, I wasn't even focused on the fact that I had just made a hundred thousand dollars, I was more focused on being excited that I had hit my goal. That was great! Returning to college life with over $100,000 in the bank was a lot of fun!

Needless to say, we did a couple of trips and I did what any normal college student would do. The next year I needed to go back to work and break some more company records and make that money back. But it was great, it really was.

### Wright

You achieved so many accomplishments at such an early age. What would you suggest for others to reach their goals quickly?

### Hillis

Unconditional confidence and accountability for reaching goals are how people get a fast start and reach goals quickly.

Unconditional confidence is something that can be taught and it can be transferred from one person to another. To have confidence one has to have a passion for focusing on what can be controlled and know that it can be done—and then just find the way to make that happen.

Everyone should have a business coach to hold him or her accountable just as Olympic athletes have coaches to hold them accountable and serve as guides to winning the gold medal. To reach goals quickly and develop unconditional confidence, people need to find someone to help them get there. Those who are qualified to be accountability coaches are (ideally):

1. Those who have been where you want to go. Why is that? They know the path to success. Learn from the mistakes of others and don't take chances that are not necessary.
2. Those who have the same goal as you have. Why is that? Competition! A good example of two people who developed competition through sharing the same goal is Mark McGwire and Sammy Sosa who had the same goal—to break the homerun record for baseball. Mr. McGwire ended up on top and broke the record, but in the end Mr. Sosa and Mr. McGwire developed a deep respect for each other and helped each other get further than they ever would have on their own.

### Wright

You played college football for two years. How did that help with your career in sales?

**Hillis**

The first time I experienced the passion I now have for doing sales training and being a motivational speaker was when I was the team captain in football and gave a motivational speech to the team before a big game. It was such a great feeling to get the whole team energized and ready to go out on the "battlefield." That was the first time I really felt the effects of what motivation can do, and saw the difference motivation can make in a player in a game.

If you have a football player who has all the talent in the world, but he's not motivated and not excited to do what he's out to do, he will not perform at optimal level. But you take that same player, get him playing with every bit of passion he has, and motivate him by getting him to understand what it means to win the game, he's going to produce and he's going to play or perform at a higher level. He will be motivated and inspired.

That's something I took away from playing football.

**Wright**

So what's up next for Dustin Hillis? What are your goals for the future?

**Hillis**

My goal is to help our company, The Southwestern Company and its sales training division Success Starts Now!™, be the number one sales training company in the world. Right now we have sales training in London, Scotland, and all throughout Europe. Here in the United States we are concentrating on big events and sales training conferences. Our next step is to focus on growing our training and coaching programs.

Right now I'm working on confidence coaching and helping people get to the next level of unconditional confidence and having consistency in their production.

We also want to provide customized training for businesses. We'll do three-day workshops (or longer if needed) and work with salespeople on a one-on-one basis.

The three services we want to provide are sales training and motivational events, personal coaching, and sales and leadership training through customized workshops to help businesses increase production.

**Wright**

What a great conversion. Dustin, I really appreciate your taking all this time with me today to answer all these questions. Sales is always on my mind all the time. I'm engaged in sales, as is almost everybody in one aspect or another. I think our readers will get a lot from what you are saying!

**Hillis**

This has been terrific and I'm looking forward to meeting each and every reader and each and every person who comes to our sales training conferences.

**Wright**

Today we have been talking with Dustin Hillis who is an expert on sales fundamentals. He teaches people tools and techniques for improving, as he calls it, "execution." He talks a lot about forming positive habits and using positive affirmations to get where we want to go. I don't know about you, but I'm going to listen to him. I think he knows what he is talking about.

Dustin, thank you so much for being with us today on *Speaking of Success.*

**Hillis**

Thank you and God bless.

## About the Author

DUSTIN HILLIS has worked with The Southwestern Company since 2002. The company has a 150-year-old sales training program and has trained hundreds of thousands of sales professionals to do direct selling. Dustin finished number one out of 3,500 salespeople worldwide during his first year with The Southwestern Company. He then finished number one every year after that and eclipsed The Southwestern Company's all-time sales record for the most product sold in a single selling season. He is a founding partner in the Southwestern Seminars professional sales training division known as Success Starts Now!™, striving to help other sales professionals break records and reach goals of their own.

**Dustin Hillis**
Southwestern Seminars (Success Starts Now!™)
2451 Atrium Way
Nashville, Tennessee 37214
Phone: 615.260.0182
E-mail: dhillis@ssnseminars.com
www.ssnseminars.com

# Chapter 4

## BARBARA SEXTON SMITH

THE INTERVIEW

### David Wright (Wright)

Today we're talking with Barbara Sexton Smith. She has helped raise more than $181 million during the past twenty years for the Fund for the Arts, Metro United Way, Louisville Olmsted Parks Conservancy, the National Conference for Christians and Jews, and the West Louisville Boys and Girls Choirs. She also founded Quick Think Inc. whose vision is, "To teach you how to get others to do what you want!" Her clients include General Electric, Nissan, Alcoa, Humana, Norton Healthcare, Brown-Forman, Steel Technologies, and Kentucky Fried Chicken. In 1996 she was nominated for the Ernst & Young Entrepreneur of the Year Award. Along the way she has also helped raise seven children and managed to make sure that 450,000 schoolchildren have an arts experience every year.

As regional manager for Wendy's International in the early eighties she was selected from 3,000 managers worldwide as Wendy's Employee of the Year. She went on to become the National Franchise Director for the Fresher Cooker.

Barbara was appointed by Mayor Jerry Abramson to serve on the Metro Louisville Air Pollution Control District Board of Directors. Her other volunteer roles include:

- President, Voter Outreach Program
- President, Downtown Police Advisory Board
- Alcoa Community Advisory Board
- Simmons College of Kentucky Board of Trustees
- Chair, Interfaith Community Hunger Project

As a member of the International Speakers Network and the National Speakers Association, Barbara is a highly sought-after speaker who inspires every audience, every time.

Barbara, welcome to *Speaking of Success.*

**Barbara Sexton Smith (Sexton Smith)**
Thanks, David. I'm glad to be here.

**Wright**
Barbara, let's get right to it. What is the most success-defining moment of your life?

**Sexton Smith**
I survived an armed robbery—successfully!

**Wright**
What happened?

**Sexton Smith**
When I was twenty-three years old I was in all my glory working as a newly hired assistant manager for Wendy's and it was almost midnight. Four teenagers were cleaning up while I was completing the nightly paperwork.

All of a sudden the place went wild—loud noises, screaming, and someone pounding on the office door screaming as loud as he could, "Open the door or I'll blow her brains out!"

I had no choice. I opened the door and there he stood. The robber who had broken into the restaurant was interested in taking whatever money we had but he was also threatening to kill the sixteen-year-old girl he was holding if I didn't do exactly everything he said. Immediately, four teenagers were on the floor as he grabbed me and began to beat the daylights out of me, screaming for the money, and telling me to open the safe.

When he hit me on the back of the head with his sawed-off shotgun, blood went everywhere and I couldn't see anything. I couldn't see the numbers on the safe and I thought, "What in the world am I going to do?"

There was a child lying on the floor next to me (I'll never forget this) who was a young Catholic boy. He was saying "Our Fathers" (repeating the Lord's Prayer) and "Hail Marys" as fast as he could go.

"What are my own beliefs?" I wondered. At the time I had no idea. To tell you the truth, David, I hadn't given it much thought. But something told me that if I didn't figure out what to do right then and get help from somebody or something not in that room, those four teenagers were going to die. I wasn't worried about myself, I was worried about them.

I placed my hand on the safe and closed my eyes and I said, "If there's a God out there somewhere, if you'll move in here and open this safe and help me do the right things and get this guy out of here, I will follow you all the days of my life." I had not turned the dial on the safe because I couldn't see clearly. I lifted my arm and the safe opened! It was a miracle.

I handed that guy the money. He had hit me twenty-two times in the back and on the head. He yanked my ponytail around one last time and made me stare right down the barrel of his shotgun. He was getting ready to pull the trigger. But then he let go and left. There are now five people living to tell that story. And that was the moment I first believed! Talk about being successful!

**Wright**

So how do you define success?

**Sexton Smith**

In my opinion, success is simply a state of mind that you achieve by enriching the lives of others every day.

**Wright**

Speaking of enriching the lives of others, I heard an amazing story about how you brought your community together to help an impoverished boys' choir. Tell us about that.

**Sexton Smith**

In August 2000 I led the journey that took the West Louisville Boys Choir to London, England, and Paris, France, to perform six concerts in spring 2001. Upon their return to America we hosted a reception for the Choir members to thank the 400 plus people who contributed money to make the trip a reality. The University of Louisville became so impressed with the project that they promised full college scholarships to every choir member who stays in the Choir through high school, meets the minimum college entrance requirements, and stays out of trouble with the law! To most of these children "college" was just a word in the dictionary!

**Wright**

Who are these children and where do they come from?

**Sexton Smith**

We're talking about thirty-one young African-American men, ages eight to eighteen, living in the poorest neighborhoods of Louisville with 80 percent coming from single parent homes.

**Wright**

How did you find out about them?

**Sexton Smith**

I'll never forget the day I met Mr. McDaniel Bluitt, founder and director of the Choir. He looked right at me and said, "Barbara, it's more than music, it's sounds of hope. We try to instill hope in the hearts of these young men, and as a child 'thinketh in his heart, so is he.'" I thought, "Oh my gosh, I know those words!" They are from the book of Proverbs—Proverbs 23:7.

**Wright**

When did Mr. Bluitt start this program?

**Sexton Smith**

The program began in 1989 as part of the Moore Temple Boys Choir. However, in 1990 he sought new ways to expand the Choir's mission by using music to reach children from Louisville's inner city. He wanted to get young African-American men off the streets after school and give them something positive to do—keep them out of harm's way. This became a crime prevention program. It wasn't long before he realized they needed school tutors as well as etiquette coaching for putting their best foot forward during concerts.

**Wright**

How often and where do they perform?

**Sexton Smith**

They perform fifty to sixty concerts every year. They have performed at the Governor's Mansion in Frankfort, Kentucky, for the Kentucky Derby Breakfast. President Bill Clinton, when in office, heard of the West Louisville Boys Choir and asked that they perform in Washington, D.C., at the unveiling of the National African-American Civil War Monument, sculpted by Ed Hamilton, another one of Louisville's heroes. When that happened, Europe called. Ed is one of the many angels on this journey!

**Wright**

What did you do after hearing Mr. Bluitt's story?

**Sexton Smith**

Lacey (my husband) and I started raising money from every corner of the community but we were still about $20,000 short when the travel agency called for final payment. I asked for forty-eight more hours and they just laughed! Lacey told me to call Bob Hill, a columnist for the *Courier-Journal,* and ask him to write about the Boys Choir's plight. When I got Bob on the phone I introduced myself and said, "Sir, I have the second greatest story to ever be told and I want to share it with you to see if you'll write about it in tomorrow's paper. How 'bout it?"

**Wright**

Are you saying you were able to get this story in the newspaper?

**Sexton Smith**

Yes. Bob's article, which appeared February 27, 2001, was titled *Sounds of Hope* and ended with his quoting me, quoting McDaniel, "If you want to help instill hope in the hearts of these young men, send money to Barbara Sexton Smith," and he put our home address on the front page of the newspaper! I'm not kidding!

**Wright**

Did anyone send money to help the cause?

**Sexton Smith**

Did they ever! The postman delivered ninety-four envelopes the next day and eighty-eight the following day. Bob forwarded an e-mail to me from the president of the University of Louisville. The e-mail said, "Bob, I've only lived here for six years and I've never heard of the West Louisville Boys Choir but this is the best article you've ever written! Call that woman and ask her to call me."

When he answered his phone I said, "Sir, this is *that woman* in the newspaper."

He proceeded to tell me that he would raise the final $20,000 we needed if I would bring the Choir to sing two songs at his next Board of Trustees meeting. Not knowing exactly how this was going to work, we showed up at Papa John's Cardinal Stadium at the appointed time.

**Wright**

Now, just how did it work?

**Sexton Smith**

Well, I told the kids if they would go in there and sing two songs those folks would give them $20,000 and save the trip. I asked them if they knew what that meant. Cormac Parker said, "Sure! That means they're paying us $10,000 a song!"

**Wright**

I guess you're telling me that the trip was saved and a good time was had by all!

**Sexton Smith**

Yes. The kids sang, the Trustees wrote checks, and 218 more envelopes arrived in our mailbox in just one week. Thirty-one young men representing Louisville, Kentucky, USA, sang their hearts out in the Louvre, at Notre Dame Cathedral, and at the church where Princess Diana and Charles were married. Thirty-one young men's lives were changed forever.

**Wright**

Barbara, you mentioned something earlier about college scholarships for these kids. How did that work?

**Sexton Smith**

When the choir returned to Louisville the president of the University was so taken with the boys' spirit that he guaranteed every one of them full scholarships to the University of Louisville. That gave us the courage to start the West Louisville Girls Choir with the same scholarship opportunities. In spring 2006, O'Farrell Head will graduate from the University of Louisville as our first choir member to do so.

These children have literally changed my life. I'll be forever grateful to each and every one of them. The greatest reward of all is not in the having but in the doing.

**Wright**

This is an amazing story of hope but something tells me you navigated the ship every step of the way on your path to success.

**Sexton Smith**

I appreciate your vote of confidence but I think first and foremost you have to believe in a greater power. To be successful you must have a vision supported by your personal mission and a set of values that you live by every day. Then you must communicate that vision while embracing humility. You then have to share your testimony and display integrity at all times. You have to be honest with yourself and others at all times. I know it's not an easy list but it's a list worth doing.

I don't think I've mentioned fun. You've got to have fun in what you're doing!

The paths we choose in life are simply vehicles through which we will accomplish our real missions. These things we call jobs are simply vehicles in which we travel to accomplish a much greater mission. Think about it.

**Wright**

Looking out for others seems to be a big theme in your life. Do you think serving others is necessary to becoming successful?

**Sexton Smith**

Absolutely! I call this servanthood.

**Wright**

What do you mean by servanthood?

**Sexton Smith**

First you have to understand that it's not about you, it's about serving others. A servant-leader is someone who leads with his or her head, heart, and hand. You must think it, feel it, and do it. You've got to put feet to your feelings.

**Wright**

How do you do that?

**Sexton Smith**

Think about what's important—what you want to be remembered for, and what kind of legacy you want to leave. Feel that in your heart with passion and take action! To sum it up, you could say that thoughts without passion are simply figments of your imagination and passion without action is simply a dream. Action changes lives.

**Wright**

How does a leader turn this into success?

**Sexton Smith**

Leaders must hire the right people. Develop them. Then race to the bottom of the pyramid to lift them up and cheer them on to greatness.

**Wright**

What does this do to the typical organizational chart?

**Sexton Smith**

Turns it upside-down! This is where the *V-Factor* comes in—V as in victory. The *V-Factor* is simply a pyramid turned upside down with a value-driven leader at the bottom. Think about that for a minute. Take the typical organizational chart with the leader standing at the top. Turn it upside down and put your hands in the air. Down at the point is your heart—that's right where you as a leader stand with all your values. A value-driven leader with a vision will be right there pushing and catching and cheering everybody else on to victory—the *V-Factor!*

**Wright**

This sounds great but how do you convince an ego-driven leader to do this?

**Sexton Smith**

Servanthood requires a huge dose of humility. Pride has no place on the path to success because "Pride goeth before destruction, and an haughty spirit before a fall" (Proverbs 16:18). Fear and pride are on opposite sides of the coin. Fear is pride's first cousin and together they'll beat you every time. Your best defense is humility and confidence.

**Wright**

Is servanthood your favorite word?

**Sexton Smith**

No, my favorite word is "hope."

**Wright**

So why hope?

**Sexton Smith**

I think one enriches the lives of others by instilling hope in their hearts. Remember, it's not about you—a heart filled with hope is a powerful thing. "As a man thinketh in his heart, so is he" (Proverbs 23:7). Hope breeds an attitude of possibility, which in turn breeds self-confidence.

**Wright**

So you think self-confidence is critical to success?

**Sexton Smith**

Absolutely!

**Wright**

Why?

**Sexton Smith**

Self-confidence is the power within that gives you the will to achieve a greater purpose. I believe we were all put on this earth to leave it a little better than how we found it. That's the universal vision.

My personal mission (everyone should have one) is to instill hope in the hearts of everyone I meet. Hope breeds confidence. A self-confident person filled with hope is someone who has only positive expectations. The word hope stands for:

> Having
> Only
> Positive
> Expectations

**Wright**

How can someone instill hope in the heart of someone else?

**Sexton Smith**

To be successful you have to be able to connect with the emotional centers of the people you are leading. Find out where they are coming from and what is important to them. It's not about you. Communicate your vision/dream in a way that reflects your understanding of their interests. Successful leaders communicate their vision in a way that makes people feel connected to the dream.

**Wright**

What do you mean by "their interests"?

**Sexton Smith**

You have to find out what their hopes and fears are. You have to show them how they can be part of something that is much bigger than they are—that's the vision. I believe people see themselves in relation to others; that's how it was all planned to be. You have to help each other develop a sense of belonging—a sense of purpose. A purpose-driven life is a life worth living.

**Wright**

How do you get this confidence you have talked so much about?

**Sexton Smith**

I think you get self-confidence by taking a chance and making it; by having faith in a greater power. Fear and confidence are opposite sides of a coin. You've got to release that fear within and replace it with self-confidence.

**Wright**

So how do you know when you're successful?

**Sexton Smith**

People define success in many different ways. When you spend most if not all your time trying to catch other people doing the right thing instead of looking for what they're doing wrong, you are successful—you get it. I learned this when I worked at Wendy's.

Many people want to evaluate success based on monetary gain and material possessions. I never did. I probably felt most successful when the president of an organization I was working for stood up and introduced me to everyone as "God's Cheerleader." I felt pretty darn good that day. That's real success in my book!

**Wright**

So who are the successful people you've known and why do you think they're successful?

**Sexton Smith**

I've been very fortunate. I have had a number of really good mentors, some of whom I will always remember. The first is Brad Ray, Chairman of the Board, Steel Technologies, a $1.3 billion company. Brad placed his employees and their families at the top of his organizational chart. When asked what he loses sleep over, he looked out over the audience and said, "Making sure that our employees and families are provided for." Brad gets it.

**Wright**

What about folks you have worked with? Has anyone been successful according to your definition?

**Sexton Smith**

The best example would be Rob Reifsnyder who served as president of Metro United Way. I got to see a real CEO in action. "CEO" in my opinion stands for Chief Expectation Officer. Rob never demanded anything. He always expected exceptional performance from everyone every day. From the maintenance crew to the senior management team, he expected everyone to surpass their goals.

As a result, Metro United Way led the nation three years in a row in highest percentage increase in dollars raised for our community and we were judged against 2,600 United Way organizations. Each year we achieved 12 percent increases. Did we enrich the lives of others? We were able to help more than 300,000 people every year, not to mention the 100,000 donors who became part of something much greater themselves.

### Wright

Sounds like Rob played a key role in your career path. Are there any women who have influenced you along the way?

### Sexton Smith

Sure. In 1999, Minx Auerbach asked me to take the lead and help her raise money to preserve and protect our precious Olmsted Park system. Minx had a reputation for asking a lot of others but you knew she was always right in there giving it her all every step of the way! As a result the Olmsted Outrageous Halloween Party has become one of the community's most highly attended events each year. It has raised more than $800,000! Hats off to Minx and all of her followers!

Joan Riehm is another one. As Deputy Mayor, Joan has been one of Louisville Mayor Jerry Abramson's greatest assets in running our great city. Joan is successful because she is the quintessential listener. She always makes time to listen to people. She immediately starts connecting people who can add value to one another.

I'll never forget the day I was waiting in the mayor's lobby for a meeting with Joan. As she came through the door she said, "Oh my gosh, Tom, you have to meet Barbara. She can really help you and you can help her." Well, Dr. Thomas Crawford, Chemistry Professor Emeritus at the University of Louisville was standing there. He had stopped by to drop off information for a program the city was co-funding with the University of Louisville.

Later that afternoon Dr. Tom called me and asked if I would help him identify fifteen dynamic people who would become the Stephen Covey certified trainers for the *Seven Habits of Highly Effective Teens.* I agreed to help him and so together, thanks to Joan's introduction, Dr. Tom and I recruited fifteen folks who are now certified Covey trainers. Through this program we have enriched the lives of more than 700 African-American youth in our community with many more to follow.

### Wright

I'm pretty impressed with the number of well-known, successful businesses headquartered in Louisville. How about some of those folks?

**Sexton Smith**

You must be talking about David Novak, Chairman of the Board of Yum! Brands Inc., the largest restaurant company in the world with more than 33,000 restaurants. Many outside the company don't realize that Yum! is an acronym and stands for You Understand Me!

David believes that if management can understand the needs of their employees, only then can they treat each employee as though he or she is the most important person in the world. He believes that employees will in turn treat customers as though they're the most important people in the world. You can read all about it in *Customer Mania,* one of Ken Blanchard's bestselling books.

**Wright**

This all sounds great but do you think the folks at Yum! really walk the talk?

**Sexton Smith**

I witnessed David walking his talk during the Fund for the Arts Employee Campaign. I was asked to host *Yum! Idol,* fashioned after the ever-so-popular *American Idol* television show. The contest lasted five days. David was seen on the front row more than once. Why? Because this event was important to his employees and he wanted them to know they were important to him. He moved the senior management team meeting across town to the service center so they could experience the excitement alongside the employees.

Successful leaders reach out to their followers. They're not afraid to meet them in their comfort zones. David is enriching the lives of others—all 804,000 plus employees worldwide.

**Wright**

Some people might say it's easy to be considered successful when you run a company that big. Can you think of someone you consider successful who is running a small company in Louisville?

**Sexton Smith**

One unsung hero is Cathy Zion. Cathy is President and Publisher of *Today's Woman,* one of the most successful women's magazines in America. Cathy publicly and privately gives all credit consistently to her staff. It's amazing! She says they're the real heroes behind the magazine's success and she's enriched their lives by trusting in their talents and lifting them up. Cathy is a good example of the *V-Factor:* Vision. Values. Victory. (Remember the upside-down pyramid?)

**Wright**

When I hear you mention vision it reminds me of those framed vision statements I see hanging on people's walls. Will you give us an example of someone who really puts it into action?

**Sexton Smith**

Sure. Steve Williams is President and CEO of Norton Healthcare in Louisville, Kentucky. Steve has done the very thing Stephen Covey teaches—to "begin with the end in mind." During his senior year in college, Steve served as my husband's legislative aide in the Kentucky State Senate.

As the story goes, one day Steve walked into Lacey's office and said, "Hey Senator, I'm going to have a career in the healthcare industry and someday I'm going to be the administrator of a major hospital. Can you give me any advice?" Steve now enriches the lives of more than 9,800 employees and their families not to mention the thousands of satisfied patients every year. Lacey must have said some pretty powerful words that day!

**Wright**

I've met a number of very motivated young people during my life. Can you think of someone just starting out who measures up to your definition of success?

**Sexton Smith**

Bristol Lansman (Coach). At twenty-one years old Bristol was named the youngest varsity field hockey coach in America at Atherton High School. As a ninth-grader she formed the first girls' high school crew team in Kentucky at the Collegiate School. Following that, as a junior at Assumption High School, she helped form the first girls' high school ice hockey team in Kentucky. She gets it. Bristol understands the power of Title IX, the federal legislation requiring sports opportunities for female athletes. She learned the importance of this from Lacey, her step-dad.

While in the State Senate, Lacey worked on the legislation that brought funding to sports programs for girls in Kentucky high schools. We have college scholarships going to female athletes all across Kentucky. These young women would have never had a chance before had it not been for Lacey and Bristol.

**Wright**

Once people become successful, are they always successful?

**Sexton Smith**

Absolutely not. Success starts over each morning when you get the wake-up call. We all play the most important sport—it's the game of life. There is only one coach. When I get the wake-up call, it's the same one you get—I don't question a thing. I get up and say, "Send me in, coach! I'm ready to play!"

Of course you have to have game rules when you're in sports. The game rules in the game of life are very simple: (1) you have to have faith and believe in yourself; (2) hope for the best; (3) you have to love yourself; and (4) you have to have rhythm—you have to be a rhythm-maker.

**Wright**

Rhythm-maker—is this how you motivate yourself to be successful every day?

**Sexton Smith**

Yes. I use the rhythm method! Now don't be misled. I'm talking about the rhythm method of *worth* control. I developed this system and anyone can follow it (everyone *should* follow it). I believe you determine your self-worth by the rhythm you choose every day. It's just that simple. You may not be able to choose what happens throughout the day but you have complete power over choosing how you will feel about it and what you will do about it.

Success is a state of mind that you choose, which is directly related to your self-worth. So you have to have a rhythm others can't knock—this is your R-O-C-K—your foundation. If you build a house on sand, it's going to end up in the sea. If you build it on a rock, it's going to stand forever. Successful people are rhythm-makers and unsuccessful people are rhythm-breakers. Your R-O-C-K is a state of mind. It's all in the big A—your attitude. Attitude is a choice.

**Wright**

So how does having a R-O-C-K help you achieve success?

**Sexton Smith**

I believe people want to follow a leader who has a strong foundation. It communicates to others that you have a vision. You're committed, you'll make tough decisions, and you have the confidence it takes to let the followers shine and share the glory when you all cross the finish line together.

This is a good place to mention *"followership"*—another one of my favorite words. You have to understand how to follow in order to be a successful leader. Leaders should constantly be helping their followers understand how what they are doing as followers fits into the vision as presented by the leader. Maybe we need to teach classes in followership. Heaven knows there are many more followers than there are leaders.

**Wright**

Is adversity important to becoming successful? If so, what role does it play?

**Sexton Smith**

I love adversity because I know that when it comes knocking, therein lies a rich opportunity for growth. You must have growth opportunities to become successful and I call these the tests we take in life. The eagle stirs up the nest so the young might learn to fly. My experience has shown that the harder the test, the greater the testimony. We really are transformed by trouble.

**Wright**

So how do you handle adversity?

**Sexton Smith**

My first reaction is to embrace it with my eyes and my ears wide open. I see opportunity in every problem, whereas a pessimist is going to see a problem in every opportunity. I also tend to look for differences among the parties because that is where the real opportunities exist. I think you have to develop a mindset to build on these differences to make the pie bigger.

**Wright**

So, who has influenced your life the most?

Sexton Smith

Mom and Dad. You can't ever forget where you came from, never. That's where I get grounded. I watched every move they made and hung onto every word they said. My dad taught me the importance of a strong work ethic and effective followership. He called it "towing the company line." And Mom always said, "Barbara Ann, if you don't have anything nice to say, don't say anything at all. Just remember, you made your bed, now sleep in it!" Mom had a way with words; that was her way of telling me to be decisive, be committed, and lift others up along the way.

My mom was living in Eastern Kentucky near Fightin' Holler when her daddy died in the coal mining camp. This caused my grandmother to send four children under the age of nine to an or- phanage in Lexington. Mom and Aunt Cleta ended up at the Ken- tucky Baptist Orphanage in Louisville. When Mom met Dad, he was studying engineering at Virginia Polytechnic Institute on a diving scholarship. His father, who had been in charge of purchasing for Westinghouse, had just passed away. Dad came to Louisville as a young man in college to visit an older brother who had moved here to work in the ammunition plant during World War II. Uncle Stuart told Dad, "There are many beautiful orphans to pick from down here!"

Uncle Stuart chose Flossie, Dad chose Mom, and when two worlds collide great things can happen!

Wright

We all know you cannot be successful by yourself. How have you engaged others along the way?

Sexton Smith

Throughout the years I have recruited, trained, and motivated thousands of volunteers who have come on board with whatever pro- ject I was working on. It's all about negotiation—it's a matter of get- ting others to do what you want.

Wright

I understand that you teach the Street-Smart Principled Negotia- tion Program in businesses all over the country. Who benefits the most?

Sexton Smith

Anyone who tries to get others to do what they want.

**Wright**

So what makes your program different?

**Sexton Smith**

Street-Smart Principled Negotiation is different because our program goal is to actually modify the negotiation behavior of the participants so as to produce increases in revenue and profitability and to produce improvements in productivity for their companies. We teach interest-based negotiation, which moves the parties away from polarization caused by positional bargaining. The parties jointly seek solutions to the issues between them. This prevents the negotiation process from becoming a contest of wills.

The program teaches ways to identify the interests of both parties and how to generate options to meet those interests. We then teach how to use standards to craft solutions that are legitimate and fair. We teach both parties how to frame positions so they can have an optimal opportunity of being agreed to.

At the end of the day participants walk away with techniques they can use immediately to become better negotiators.

**Wright**

How will they benefit? What's in it for them?

**Sexton Smith**

First of all they will use the R.E.A.L. ROI system of measurement to improve results that we've developed. They will:

1. Own a practical framework to negotiate with every day,
2. Grow their business and increase their productivity,
3. Sharpen their negotiation skills,
4. Master change and catapult effectiveness,
5. Build better relationships,
6. Learn how to solve their own toughest problems, and
7. Make more durable deals.

**Wright**

What a great conversation. I have learned a lot here today and I really do appreciate this time you have spent with me here answering all these questions. I've been taking copious notes and I'm really learning.

Do you have any final thoughts?

**Sexton Smith**

Yes. Success is a state of mind that you achieve by enriching the lives of others. It's not about you. You define your own success. The feeling and thinking—that's the easy part, but it is what we finally choose to do that makes all the difference, not just for those whom we serve but for ourselves. Our actions define who we are and what we think is important.

We must get and give hope. We were all put on this earth to leave it a little better than how we found it. Now, go do it and do it today!

**Wright**

Today we've been talking with Barbara Sexton Smith. Over the past twenty years she has been responsible for helping to raise more than $181 million for the arts, education, health and human services, and the never-ending fight against racism, bias, and bigotry. In all of her pursuits—civic as well as business—she is a team-builder, a team leader, a motivator, an innovator, and it could be argued that she personifies entrepreneurship.

Barbara, thank you so much for being with us today on *Speaking of Success.*

## About the Author

BARBARA SEXTON SMITH is among the top ten speakers for the International Speakers Network and is a nominee for the 2007 Woman of Achievement Award. She was named the 2003 Community Angel by *Today's Woman*. She and her husband, Lacey, received the 2006 McDaniel Bluitt Hope Award for instilling hope in the hearts of so many young people.

**Barbara Sexton Smith**
Quick Think Seminars
711 West Main Street
Louisville, Kentucky 40202
Phone: 502.583.0467
E-mail: barbara@barbarasextonsmith.com
www.barbarasextonsmith.com

# Chapter 5

## DR. STEPHEN R. COVEY

### David Wright (Wright)

We're talking today with Dr. Stephen R. Covey, cofounder and vice-chairman of Franklin Covey Company, the largest management company and leadership development organization in the world. Dr. Covey is perhaps best known as the author of *The 7 Habits of Highly Effective People* which is ranked as a number one best seller by the *New York Times*, having sold more than fourteen million copies in thirty-eight languages throughout the world. Dr. Covey is an internationally respected leadership authority, family expert, teacher, and organizational consultant. He has made teaching principle-centered living and principle-centered leadership his life's work. Dr. Covey is the recipient of the Thomas More College Medallion for Continuing Service to Humanity and has been awarded four honorary doctorate degrees. Other awards given Dr. Covey include the Sikh's 1989 International Man of Peace award, the 1994 International Entrepreneur of the Year award, *Inc.* magazine's Services Entrepreneur of the Year award, and in 1996 the National Entrepreneur of the Year Lifetime Achievement award for Entrepreneurial leadership. He has also been recognized as one of *Time* magazine's twenty-five most influential Americans and one of Sales and Marketing Management's top twenty-five power brokers. Dr. Covey earned his undergraduate degree from the University of Utah, his MBA from Harvard, and completed his doctorate at Brigham Young University. While at Brigham Young he served as assistant to the President and was also a professor of business management and organizational behavior.

Dr. Covey, welcome to *Speaking of Success!*

**Dr. Stephen Covey (Covey)**
Thank you.

**Wright**
Dr. Covey, most companies make decisions and filter them down through their organization. You, however, state that no company can succeed until individuals within it succeed. Are the goals of the company the result of the combined goals of the individuals?

**Covey**
Absolutely, because if people aren't on the same page, they're going to be pulling in different directions. To teach this concept, I frequently ask large audiences to close their eyes and point north, and then to keep pointing and open their eyes and they find themselves pointing all over the place. I say to them, "Tomorrow morning if you want a similar experience, ask the first ten people you meet in your organization what the purpose of your organization is and you'll find it's a very similar experience. They'll point all over the place." When people have a different sense of purpose and values, every decision that is made from then on is governed by those. There's no question that this is one of the fundamental causes of misalignment, low trust, interpersonal conflict, interdepartmental rivalry, people operating on personal agendas, and so forth.

**Wright**
Is that mostly a result of the inability to communicate from the top?

**Covey**
That's one aspect, but I think it's more fundamental. There's an inability to involve people—an unwillingness. Leaders may communicate what their mission and their strategy is, but that doesn't mean

there's any emotional connection to it. Mission statements that are rushed and then announced are soon forgotten. They become nothing more than just a bunch of platitudes on the wall that mean essentially nothing and even create a source of cynicism and a sense of hypocrisy inside the culture of an organization.

## Wright

How do companies ensure survival and prosperity in these tumultuous times of technological advances, mergers, downsizing, and change?

## Covey

I think that it takes a lot of high trust in a culture that has something that doesn't change—principles—at its core. There are principles that people agree upon that are valued. It gives a sense of stability. Then you have the power to adapt and be flexible when you experience these kinds of disruptive new economic models or technologies that come in and sideswipe you. You don't know how to handle them unless you have something you can depend upon. If people have not agreed to a common set of principles that guide them and a common purpose, then they get their security from the outside and they tend to freeze the structure, systems, and processes inside and they cease becoming adaptable. They don't change with the changing realities of the new marketplace out there and gradually they become obsolete.

## Wright

I was interested in one portion of your book *The 7 Habits of Highly Effective People* where you talk about behaviors. How does an individual go about the process of replacing ineffective behaviors with effective ones?

## Covey

I think that for most people it usually requires a crisis that humbles them to become aware of their ineffective behaviors. If there's not a crisis the tendency is to perpetuate those behaviors and not change. You don't have to wait until the marketplace creates the crisis for you. Have everyone accountable on a 360 degree basis to everyone else they interact with—with feedback either formal or informal—where they are getting data as to what's happening. They will then start to realize that the consequences of their ineffective behavior require them to be humble enough to look at that behavior and to adopt new, more effective ways of doing things. Sometimes people can be stirred up to this if you just appeal to their conscience—to their inward sense of what is right and wrong. A lot of people sometimes know inwardly they're doing wrong, but the culture doesn't necessarily discourage them from continuing that. They either need feedback from people, or they need feedback from the marketplace, or they need feedback from their conscience. Then they can begin to develop a step-by-step process of replacing old habits with new, better habits.

**Wright**

It's almost like saying, "Let's make all the mistakes in the laboratory before we put this thing in the air."

**Covey**

Right; and I also think what is necessary is a paradigm shift, which is analogous to having a correct map, say of a city or of a country. If people have an inaccurate paradigm of life, of other people, and of themselves it really doesn't make much difference what their behavior or habits or attitudes are. What they need is a correct paradigm—a correct map—that describes what's going on. For instance, in the Middle Ages they used to heal people through bloodletting. It wasn't until Samuel Weiss and Pasteur and other empirical scientists discovered the germ theory that they realized for the first time they weren't dealing with the real issue. They realized why women preferred to use midwives who washed rather than doctors who didn't wash. They gradually got a new paradigm. Once you've got a new paradigm then your behavior and your attitude flows directly from it. If you have a bad paradigm or a bad map, let's say of a city, there's no way, no matter what your behavior or your habits or your attitudes are—how positive they are—you'll never be able to find the location you're looking for. This is why I believe that to change paradigms is far more fundamental than to work on attitude and behavior.

**Wright**

One of your seven habits of highly effective people is to begin with the end in mind. If circumstances change and hardships or miscalculation occurs, how does one view the end with clarity?

Covey

Many people think to begin with the end in mind means that you have some fixed definition of a goal that's accomplished and if changes come about you're not going to adapt to them. Instead, the "end in mind" you begin with is that you are going to create a flexible culture of high trust so that no matter what comes along you are going to do whatever it takes to accommodate that new change or that new reality and maintain a culture of high performance and high trust. You're talking more in terms of values and overall purposes that don't change, rather than specific strategies or programs that will have to change to accommodate the changing realities in the marketplace.

Wright

In this time of mistrust between people, corporations, and nations for that matter, how do we create high levels of trust?

Covey

That's a great question and it's complicated because there are so many elements that go into the creating of a culture of trust. Obviously the most fundamental one is just to have trustworthy people. But that is not sufficient because what if the organization itself is misaligned? For instance, what if you say you value cooperation but you really reward people for internal competition? Then you have a systemic or a structure problem that creates low trust inside the culture even though the people themselves are trustworthy. This is one of the insights of Edward Demming and the work he did. That's why he said that most problems are not personal; they're systemic. They're common caused. That's why you have to work on structure, systems, and processes to make sure that they institutionalize principle-centered values. Otherwise you could have good people with bad systems and you'll get bad results.

When it comes to developing interpersonal trust between people, it is made up of many, many elements such as taking the time to listen to other people, to understand them, and to see what is important to them. What we think is important to another may only be important to us, not to another. It takes empathy. You have to make and keep promises to them. You have to treat them with kindness and courtesy. You have to be completely honest and open. You have to live up to your commitments. You can't betray them behind their back. You can't badmouth them behind their back and sweet-talk them to their face. That will send out vibes of hypocrisy and it will be detected. You have to learn to apologize when you make mistakes, to admit mistakes, and to also get feedback going in every direction as much as possible. It doesn't necessarily require formal forums; it requires trust between people that will be open with each other and give each other feedback.

**Wright**

My mother told me to do a lot of what you're saying now, but it seems like when I got in business I simply forgot.

**Covey**

Sometimes we forget, but sometimes culture doesn't nurture it. That's why I say unless you work with the institutionalizing—that means formalizing into structure, systems, and processes the values—you will not have a nurturing culture. You have to constantly work on that. This is one of the big mistakes organizations make. They think trust is simply a function of being honest. That's only one small aspect. It's an important aspect, obviously, but there are so many other elements that go into the creation of a high trust culture.

**Wright**

"Seek first to understand then to be understood" is another of your seven habits. Do you find that people try to communicate without really understanding what other people want?

**Covey**

Absolutely. The tendency is to project out of our own autobiography—our own life, our own value system—onto other people, thinking we know what they want. So we don't really listen to them. We pretend to listen, but we really don't listen from within their frame of reference. We listen from within our own frame of reference and we're really preparing our reply rather than seeking to understand. This is a very common thing. In fact very few people have had any training in seriously listening. They're trained in how to read, write, and speak, but not to listen.

Reading, writing, speaking, and listening are the four modes of communication and they represent about two-thirds to three-fourths of our waking hours. About half of that time is spent listening, but it's the one skill people have not been trained in. People have had all this training in the other forms of communication. In a large audience of

1,000 people you wouldn't have more than twenty people who have had more than two weeks of training in listening. Listening is more than a skill or a technique so that you're listening within another frame of reference. It takes tremendous courage to listen because you're at risk when you listen. You don't know what's going to happen; you're vulnerable.

**Wright**

Sales gurus always tell me that the number one skill in selling is listening.

**Covey**

Yes—listening from within the customer's frame of reference. That is so true. You can see that it takes some security to do that because you don't know what's going to happen.

**Wright**

With our *Speaking of Success!* talk show and book we're trying to encourage people in our audience to be better, to live better, and be more fulfilled by listening to the examples of our guests. Is there anything or anyone in your life that has made a difference for you and helped you to become a better person?

**Covey**

I think the most influential people in my life have been my parents. I think that what they modeled was not to make comparisons and harbor jealousy or to seek recognition. They were humble people. I remember my mother one time when we were going up in an elevator and the most prominent person in the state was in the elevator. She knew him, but she spent her time talking to the elevator operator. I was just a little kid and I was so awed by this person and I said to my mom, "Why didn't you talk to the important person?" She said, "I was. I had never met him." They were really humble, modest people who were focused on service and other people rather than on themselves. I think they were very inspiring models to me.

**Wright**

In almost every research paper that anyone I've ever read writes about people who influenced their lives, in the top five people, three of them are teachers. My seventh grade English teacher was the greatest teacher I ever had and influenced me to no end.

**Covey**

Would it be correct to say that she saw in you probably some qualities of greatness you didn't even see in yourself?

**Wright**

Absolutely.

**Covey**

That's been my general experience that the key aspect of a mentor or a teacher is someone who sees in you potential that you don't even see in yourself. They treat you accordingly and eventually you come to see it in yourself. That's my definition of leadership or influence—communicating people's worth and potential so clearly that they are inspired to see it in themselves.

**Wright**

Most of my teachers treated me as a student, but she treated me with much more respect than that. As a matter of fact, she called me Mr. Wright in the seventh grade. I'd never been addressed by anything but a nickname. I stood a little taller; she just made a tremendous difference. Do you think there are other characteristics that mentors seem to have in common?

**Covey**

I think they are first of all good examples in their own personal lives. Their personal lives and their family lives are not all messed up—they come from a base of good character. They also are usually very confident and they take the time to do what your teacher did to you—to treat you with uncommon respect and courtesy.

They also, I think, explicitly teach principles rather than practices so that rules don't take the place of human judgment. You gradually come to have faith in your own judgment in making decisions because of the affirmation of such a mentor. Good mentors care about you—you can feel the sincerity of their caring. It's like the expression, "I don't care how much you know until I know how much you care."

**Wright**

Most people are fascinated with the new television shows about being a survivor. What has been the greatest comeback that you've made from adversity in your career or your life?

**Covey**

When I was in grade school I experienced a disease in my legs. It caused me to use crutches for a while. I tried to get off them fast and get back. The disease wasn't corrected yet so I went back on crutches for another year. The disease went to the other leg and I went on for another year. It essentially took me out of my favorite thing—athletics—and it took me more into being a student. So that was kind of a life-defining experience which at the time seemed very negative, but has proven to be the basis on which I've focused my life—being more of a learner.

**Wright**

Principle-centered learning is basically what you do that's different from anybody I've read or listened to.

**Covey**

The concept is embodied in the far-eastern expression, "Give a man a fish, you feed him for the day; teach him how to fish, you feed him for a lifetime." When you teach principles that are universal and timeless, they don't belong to just any one person's religion or to a particular culture or geography. They seem to be timeless and universal like the ones we've been talking about here: trustworthiness, honesty, caring, service, growth, and development. These are universal principles. If you focus on these things then little by little people become independent of you and then they start to believe in themselves and their own judgment becomes better. You don't need as many rules. You don't need as much bureaucracy and as many controls and you can empower people.

The problem in most business operations today—and not just business but non-business—is that they're using the industrial model in an information age. Arnold Toynbee, the great historian, said, "You can pretty well summarize all of history in four words: nothing fails like success." The industrial model was based on the asset of the machine. The information model is based on the asset of the person—the knowledge worker. It's an altogether different model. But the machine model was the main asset of the twentieth century. It enabled productivity to increase fifty times. The new asset is intellectual and social capital—the qualities of people and the quality of the relationship they have with each other. Like Toynbee said, "Nothing fails like success." The industrial model does not work in an information age. It requires a focus on the new wealth, not capital and material things.

A good illustration that demonstrates how much we were into the industrial model, and still are, is to notice where people are on the balance sheet. They're not found there. Machines are found there. Machines become investments. People are on the profit and loss statement and people are expenses. Think of that—if that isn't blood-letting.

**Wright**

It sure is.

When you consider the choices you've made down through the years, has faith played an important role in your life?

**Covey**

It has played an extremely important role. I believe deeply that we should put principles at the center of our lives, but I believe that God is the source of those principles. I did not invent them. I get credit sometimes for some of the Seven Habits material and some of the other things I've done, but it's really all based on principles that have been given by God to all of His children from the beginning of time. You'll find that you can teach these same principles from the sacred texts and the wisdom literature of almost any tradition. I think the ultimate source of that is God and that is one thing you can absolutely depend upon—in God we trust.

**Wright**

If you could have a platform and tell our audience something you feel would help them or encourage them, what would you say?

**Covey**

I think I would say to put God at the center of your life and then prioritize your family. No one on their deathbed ever wished they spent more time at the office.

**Wright**

That's right. We have come down to the end of our program and I know you're a busy person, but I could talk with you all day Dr. Covey.

**Covey**

It's good to talk with you as well and to be a part of this program. It looks like an excellent one that you've got going on here.

**Wright**

Thank you.

We have been talking today with Dr. Stephen R. Covey, co-founder and vice-chairman of Franklin Covey Company. He's also the author of *The 7 Habits of Highly Effective People,* which has been ranked as a number one bestseller by the *New York Times*, selling more than fourteen million copies in thirty-eight languages.

Dr. Covey, thank you so much for being with us today on *Speaking of Success!*

**Covey**

Thank you for the honor of participating.

## About The Author

Stephen R. Covey was recognized in 1996 as one of Time magazine's twenty-five most influential Americans and one of Sales and Marketing Management's top twenty-five power brokers. Dr. Covey is the author of several acclaimed books, including the international bestseller, The 7 Habits of Highly Effective People. It has sold more than fifteen million copies in thirty-eight languages throughout the world. Other bestsellers authored by Dr. Covey include First Things First, Principle-Centered Leadership (with sales exceeding one million), and The 7 Habits of Highly Effective Families.

Dr. Covey's newest book, The 8th Habit: From Effectiveness to Greatness, which was released in November 2004, rose to the top of several bestseller lists, including New York Times, Wall Street Journal, USA Today, Money, Business Week, and Amazon.com and Barnes & Noble. The 8th Habit . . . has sold more than 360,000 copies.

Dr. Covey earned his undergraduate degree from the University of Utah, his MBA from Harvard, and completed his doctorate at Brigham Young University. While at Brigham Young University, he served as assistant to the President and was also a professor of business management and organizational behavior. He received the National Fatherhood Award in 2003, which, as the father of nine and grandfather of forty-four, he says is the most meaningful award he has ever received.

Dr. Covey currently serves on the board of directors for the Points of Light Foundation. Based in Washington, D.C., the Foundation, through its partnership with the Volunteer Center National Network, engages and mobilizes millions of volunteers from all walks of life—businesses, nonprofits, faith-based organizations, low-income communities, families, youth, and older adults—to help solve serious social problems in thousands of communities.

Dr. Stephen R. Covey
www.stephencovey.com

# *Chapter 6*

## KIRK WEISLER

**David Wright (Wright)**

Are you looking for insights that magnify your power to inspire your people and *invite* them to move to higher ground? Then meet Kirk Weisler, an amazingly creative and insightful corporate sage, speaker, and author whose contagious energy and passion jumps off the stage—and the pages of his books—straight into your heart. His life mission is to imbue organizations with deeper meaning, greater purpose, passion and, *fun!*

Author of the best *smelling* book, *Dog Poop Initiative,* Kirk Weisler is *the* Chief Morale Officer and expert in creating outrageously cool, committed, company cultures.

So let's get started.

I have heard—and heard of—some of Kirk's, presentations: "The How and the Wow and the Flight of the Cow," "It's all about the Love," "Motivator in Black," and "Little Big Leadership."

Are we expecting a normal interview? Nope. In fact, Kirk has already told me that we will discover how level five business leaders are dramatically enhancing the power and effectiveness of their company cultures with "Milk and Cookie Management" and "Love Note Leadership." We will also explore other fun things leaders can do *right now* to create a more positive, connected, and outrageously cool company culture.

I can tell you're ready, Kirk, so let's go!

### Kirk Weisler (Weisler)

That's right, David. My goal is that your listeners and readers will leave this interview with at least three things they can implement right now—no additional tools to buy, no consultants to hire, and best of all *no permission needed.* In other words, no excuses for not making our world of work better right now—for our people and ourselves.

### Wright

The context is culture and the mission is to nurture it, improve it, and inspire the people who sustain it and in the process, create cool, connected, company cultures, right?

### Weisler

Right on, David. I call it cultural leadership.

### Wright

In a sentence or two, would you define organizational culture for our readers?

### Weisler

Sure thing. It's what really happens around here and what that feels like. It's what *really is,* not what we hope or pretend that it is.

### Wright

"It's what it really is." Hum, I like that.

### Weisler

Our organization's culture is that feeling that comes from what we really do around here *and the spirit in which it is done.* It supersedes what we say we are and reflects who we really are. It eclipses our pithy posted mission statements and validates or voids our vision statements. It is what our company feels like. It is what our company sounds like. It is manifest in our prevailing attitudes and behaviors. It is in the language we use, the types of stories we tell; it is the real *spirit* of the place. This feeling—this spirit—is as felt by those outside the company as it is experienced and felt by those inside the company.

Even more important than what culture is, is what it does. It affects every measurable outcome.

Visualize, David, a sliding scale. At one end is joy, emotional commitment, camaraderie, connection, engagement, all the good stuff that good leaders are always striving for, and on the other end is disengagement, discontent, discord and disconnection—even despair—the bad stuff good leaders are always striving against. Every organization's culture is somewhere on this scale, passively moving down the scale in response to circumstances or actively moving up the scale as a result of the focused, deliberate attention their leaders give their company culture. One employee called it "retention guided by intention." I call it Cultural Leadership.

**Wright**

So you're either headed from "Good to Great" or—

**Weisler**

Or sliding from "Good to Grey."

**Wright**

Okay then Kirk, how about taking us to "great" with some things leaders can do—today—to transform their corporate culture and keep them growing in the right direction.

**Weisler**

Yes. There are a dozen things that really work—and begin to work immediately. In fact, today I will give you three of my top ten favorite activities that help leaders create and nurture outrageously cool cultures. Number one: serve milk and cookies. Number two: write love notes. And number three: read to your people.

**Wright**

Read to them? Read what to them?

**Weisler**

David, the "what" doesn't matter nearly so as the "how." Certainly you should read something that is relevant and inspiring. Read them something you know and love and want to share because it moved you emotionally, energetically, or creatively. It doesn't need to be overtly connected to their daily tasks; in fact, it doesn't necessarily need to be linked to their work at all. Remember, you aren't reading to them to try to fix them, you are reading to awaken or nurture the seeds of greatness inside them and inspire their initiative and creativity.

I often read books to my teams at work or corporate audiences that you would never find in the business section of the bookstore—or even the self-help section, for that matter.

**Wright**

What kind of books are we talking about then?

**Weisler**

I prefer reading children's stories like, *Sneetches, Sir Kevin of Devin,* and *Oh, the places you'll go . . .*

**Wright**

Sounds like fun, how do adult executives react to that?

**Weisler**

They absolutely love it. Whether it is at a corporate executive retreat, a conference keynote with hundreds of people, or a ten-person weekly staff meeting, adults love to be read to. You can count on your team cynics and naysayers to roll their eyes when you first start reading a Dr. Seuss book, but you can also count on the majority of your people loving it. In many cases they will demand that it be done more often. Furthermore, I can promise that when you consistently do this, your cynics will be the first to complain if you were to stop.

**Wright**

Wow! Reading a children's book is easy. I could do that.

**Weisler**

Exactly. But will you? I don't mean to sound blunt, but the road to poor culture is paved with good intentions of things that could have been done but were not. There are so many things that *could* be so easily done, but it is developing the habit of doing it that actually gets it done. Cultural leadership requires us to invite people to actually commit to doing these new things, engage in new behaviors, and grow in the process.

The direct nature of the "will you?" question helps to immediately assess someone's willingness and faith in you and your leadership. So it's not a question of if you *can;* rather, it is a question of if you *will.*

*So,* David, *will you* take two to seven minutes and read to the wonderful people you work with—and *will you* do it in your next staff meeting?

**Wright**

You got me. And, yes, I will. I am actually excited to. Does it need to be a children's book?

**Weisler**

It could be; but remember, the *how* is more important that the *what.* Some of the favorite books I read to my team at home, and to audiences abroad, are "grown-up books" that are fun quick reads but also have depth and inspiration—books like *Raving Fans, The Big Moo, Q B Q, Who Moved My Cheese,* and even from those big, fat intimidating books such as *The Goal, Good to Great, Leadership Challenge,* we can easily find exciting vignettes loaded with insights that uplift, inform, and inspire. Remember, read your selections with the same excitement you felt when you first "got it"—with the same enthusiasm you would share any exciting discovery. When you do, I promise you that great things will happen.

**Wright**

Great things like—?

**Weisler**

Like what happened to my friend and client, Brenda. Brenda shifted her company culture in one day. Here's what happened. She walked into her weekly staff meeting and said, "Listen to this! I have been reading this really cool book on change. Before we jump into today's agenda, I just have to read this to you."

She opened the book *Who Moved my Cheese,* and enthusiastically began to read. In moments, her team knew the characters and could identify with them. They listened intently as she read right up to a "cliffhanger spot" then, looking at her watch, she stopped abruptly. "Well, that's all we have time for right now, but it's a great story. I loved it, thanks for letting me share a bit of it with you."

A member of the team pled with her to finish the story, or at least tell them what happens when the character re-enters the scary maze.

Brenda declined, but said that anyone who wished to could stop by and borrow the book. She told them she even had an extra copy they could borrow. What do you think happened?

**Wright**

Someone came and borrowed the book?

**Weisler**

More than that. By noon, *seven* people came and borrowed the book.

**Wright**

How do seven people borrow one book?

**Weisler**

I had told Brenda what to expect and she had the extra copies waiting in her desk drawer.

**Wright**

Ah ha, smart lady (smart Kirk). Here's another question. I might know the answer, but let me ask it anyway. How did reading that book shift the company culture in one day?

**Weisler**

Well, obviously, this didn't move her culture from one end of the scale to other, but this did invite and move it in the right direction. The cumulative effect of consistently doing what Brenda did is where the power is. By reading to her team, and inspiring them to read she gave them something in common. You see, cultures are established and maintained by the things they have in common, things like stories—true stories, legends, histories, fables, parables—stories that illustrate and prove values, behavioral standards, and a shared and common language—especially a common language. These stories can be intentionally installed into your culture from books, the experiences from your cultural leaders, or from inspiring, internal examples. However it happens, and the principles they illustrate, they must be told deliberately and repetitiously to drive these stories into the heart of your culture. You will know you have succeeded, and your culture has shifted, when you hear echoes of those stories coming back to you in the everyday language of your company.

The next day someone on Brenda's team was wandering around the office looking for something he had misplaced and a co-worker walked up and said, "Are you looking for your cheese?"

Immediately, another called out from the next cubicle, laughing, "Too bad, I moved it!"

Bingo! Their shared and common experience and values had shifted to a different level and style of thinking. The office culture had shifted and their language immediately reflected that shift. By the way, their humor indicated a certain level of acceptance and adoption of the change in culture and language.

### Wright

Yes. I get it. The culture immediately shifted through stories. Like the one you just told me. But I would assume it could shift right back once the novelty of the story wore off, right?

### Weisler

Right. Absolutely. Good catch. But this wasn't a one-time experience. Brenda kept up the practice—she made it a tradition. And remember, it went beyond just reading to them. Brenda read to them with passion and purpose. You have to let your enthusiasm for your favorite books become contagious so that you inspire them to want to read more themselves—and share what they read with each other.

No one would argue that it is more fun to work with someone who is in a state of growth and development than it is to work with someone who is stagnant. Green wood is more flexible and much less likely to burn (out) than deadwood.

Gallup's wonderful research in the area of "employee engagement" clearly indicates that a key element that must be present for employee engagement to be at its zenith is personal and professional development.

The greatest single thing supervisors and CEOs can do to get their people into a state of growth and development is to be in one themselves. One of the best ways I know of to accomplish this is to read what great and inspiring authors like Dr. Seuss or Jim Collins have to say and then share those thoughts and ideas, not by preaching your new discoveries and ideas, but by simply doing what Brenda did—reading to your team.

### Wright

I love it Kirk, share another example with us.

**Weisler**

I have hundreds of e-mails and letters from company leaders like Brenda telling me how they made it happen; but let me tell you a story about how it *didn't* work.

It is also a true story and tragically it is one of many. A particular company had some big changes coming. (Who doesn't?) In a well intended but poorly executed attempt to prepare their people for this change, they decided it would be good to have everyone read the aforementioned best selling book on change, *Who Moved My Cheese?*

**Wright**

Like Brenda did—

**Weisler**

No, not quite. This company's idea was awesome, but their implementation was awful. Like so many companies, they lacked the personal buy-in that is inherent in the kind of contagious cultural leadership that Brenda demonstrated when she read to her people.

This other company just handed out the book and expected their people to read it. They purchased hundreds of copies and laid them on people's keyboards so they would discover them when they arrived at work the next morning.

**Wright**

So, everyone got a book, right?

**Weisler**

Yes, but the objective wasn't for them to get the book. The objective was for them to get the message—the message that was in the book. The company wanted and needed to get their people to *read* the book to get the book's powerful message. It wasn't just to get the books into their hands but to get the book's message into their hearts—and their minds—so it would affect their language and behavioral responses thereby producing measurable, positive effects. That's how cultural leaders create cultural change.

**Wright**

I can see why they didn't read it. They show up, find it on their keyboard, and most likely view it as another task on their plates that are already too full or as another stumbling attempt by management to "improve morale around here" or maybe even some kind of subtle criticism that they needed to be more "positive" or something like that.

**Weisler**

Exactly right, David; and, well, their positive intent to get their people to start reading uplifting and inspirational books didn't happen. They spent thousands of dollars on books that few even opened and even fewer read. The book simply got moved from their desktops to their shelf tops—to be read later, if ever. The company didn't affect the mindset of their culture, let alone the heart-set. They totally failed to help their people prepare for change.

**Wright**

Okay. Here's what I've got so far. You can shift your company culture upward in one day—or at least start the process—by reading to your people, not by reading just anything, but by reading something that matters. Read with passion so you entice them to read it themselves—and maybe even to each other—so it sinks into the heart and shows up in an enhanced company culture. Do I have it right?

**Weisler**

Yes; and what else did you get out of this, David?

**Wright**

What do you mean?

**Weisler**

Knowing is not enough, we must—

**Wright**

Oh yes, *act.* I will read to my people at our next staff meeting here at Insight Publishing.

**Weisler**

Great, they'll love you for it.

**Wright**

Really, I'm going to do it. Heck, I'm excited to do it. It's such a simple idea, yet obviously effective. But we aren't done, yet. You said you had *three* ideas you would share with us that would make an immediate change. Do you have time for a couple more? Actually, I'm not letting you leave here until you do anyway. You said something about love notes and milk and cookies. What is that all about, oh sage of simplicity? Are these also things I can do right here, right now, with my own staff?

**Weisler**

You sure can David; in fact, anyone can. We'll end with the cookies and milk. Let's go first to the love because it's all about the love. Are you feelin' the love?

**Wright**

Yes, I'm feeling it!

**Weisler**

David, one very easy, yet incredibly effective thing any leader can do right now is to simply write a "love note."

**Wright**

A love note? Well, this is a business book so obviously you're not talking romance. I am sure you're talking cultural context, right?

**Weisler**

Of course. Company culture is the crucible of production and profit; the birthplace of all desired organizational results—particularly long-range results. Culture is the heart of the organization. People are the heart of the culture and, well, the heart is the heart of the people—their emotions and their feelings are what drive them and keep them going over the long-haul.

If you operate with the understanding that culture drives your company and at the core of culture is the individual and at the core of the individual is the heart, then you must realize that if you are going to change your company culture you must start with the heart of the individual. Love notes are an easy, quick, and powerful way to get you closer to the heart of the individual—the heartbeat of your culture.

A love note in the context of our discussion is simply a handwritten note of appreciation written by anyone in the culture to anyone else in the culture. The key elements of the note are: first, that someone cares enough to write it; second, that it is descriptive or specific as it conveys what or who is appreciated and why; and third, that it is given in the spirit of genuine appreciation. Oh, and the signature, that's important too.

**Wright**

The signature?

**Weisler**

Some notes are powerful if they are left anonymously, some are more effective if they are signed by the entire team, and others are better if they are signed individually. It depends on the situation.

**Wright**

How does a person know what is best?

**Weisler**

You usually just know. Follow your instincts. You see, David, love notes are important because of the power they have to meet one of the greatest human needs we know of: the need to feel loved, recognized, and appreciated—the feeling that I matter, that I make a difference, and that what I *do* is worthwhile and worth noticing and therefore *I* am worthwhile and worth noticing.

This is a very important principle or truth and we each have the ability to use its power to bless more lives, more often. We can start *right now* by simply taking a few moments to write a genuine note of appreciation for someone in our world or work—or our world in general.

My editor proudly told me he has a box of really classy thank-you notes in his top desk drawer. I asked him why? He said "so I can give them to people." I asked him how long they had been in his desk drawer. He gulped in embarrassment and said, "Oh, I guess I haven't been giving them out enough."

**Wright**

Well, that put him on the spot.

**Weisler**

My question was spontaneous and was not meant to put him on the spot and while I didn't mean to embarrass him (he is tough he can take it), it was on target. He told me the next day that he got them out immediately and used them to thank several people for their contributions and support.

When discussing this principle in trainings and keynotes, I commonly ask my audiences if they have ever received a handwritten note of appreciation from a co-worker or supervisor. Usually there are a good number who raise their hands, but there are far too many who do not.

I then ask how many have received such notes have kept them for more than one year, five years, ten years. Most of the hands that were raised remain so. It's common to find people who have kept these "love" notes for over twenty years. One lady told me she kept one of hers tucked away in a desk drawer for over twenty-seven years—almost her entire professional life.

Not only do people keep these notes, they treasure these genuinely written *specific* words of appreciation as though they are written in gold. They keep them in special folders and boxes and re-read them again and again. These notes seem to get sweeter with each reading.

## Wright

There is a lot of power in this, isn't there?

## Weisler

There sure is, David; because matters of the heart such as genuine gratitude and recognition are almost sacred. Gallup's research tells us that for a company culture to be at its optimum, most positive and productive level, meaningful recognition on a personal level must occur every seven days.

## Wright

What? Every week? What company can do that? That's an awful lot!

## Weisler

It is a lot, but it is worth a lot. And you are also right, few companies do it—and that is a sad thing. Love notes are such an easy, inexpensive way to immediately enhance morale and productivity and practically no one does it. Many organizations have annual recognition events where a few select employees are acknowledged. Some have quarterly events; but none of these events even begin to fill the need that we human beings have for acknowledgement, not just "attaboys," but real constructive recognition of specific things we do or specific traits we have that enhance others.

**Wright**

So what kind of event should a company have and how often?

**Weisler**

"Events" aren't going to solve the problem. The fact is, the need for acknowledgement that Gallup describes cannot be met at an institutional level. It can only be met at a personal level—the intimate individual level. It does not need to be formal. In fact, informal works better anyway. At this interpersonal level, meaningful recognition doesn't need to come from a particular person or place, it just needs to happen. And the recognition doesn't need to be public; in fact, most people prefer personal, handwritten notes over the more showy but less meaningful organizational certificates and plaques.

**Wright**

What do you say to the people in your audiences who have never received any love notes at all?

**Weisler**

That's easy. I remind them of a couple of important truths. First, it's not about them, it's about others. Second, you get what you give. There is a close correlation between what we sow and what we reap.

**Wright**

The law of the harvest?

**Weisler**

Exactly. As cultural leaders our mission is to invite them and commit them in the strongest terms possible to improve their culture by taking action. We challenge them to do a very simple thing: ask themselves what would it feel like for them to find a genuine, specific, and heartfelt handwritten note or e-mail waiting for them at the beginning of a workday. If the answer is, "It would make me feel great," or "energized" or "more focused" or "more productive," then I suggest that they let that answer inspire them to action so they can give that great feeling to someone else and watch—and *feel*—what happens.

**Wright**

I know I'd love to get one . . .

**Weisler**

So—

**Wright**

So I'd better get to writing them if I expect to get any.

**Weisler**

Good, but be sure to write them to bless lives, not so you will receive one for yourself. It is far more powerful when we are doing it with no thought of what we might get from the experience ourselves.

**Wright**

Got it. You are right, of course. And the great thing, Kirk, about what you are suggesting is that the times we serve in the spirit you describe are among the most personally rewarding times of our lives.

**Weisler**

Exactly. So David, will you commit to writing at least one note of recognition for three members of your staff this week?

**Wright**

I will!

**Weisler**

I promise you that when you do, your culture will shift to higher ground.

**Wright**

I believe it.

**Weisler**

Now, are you now ready for "milk and cookies"?

**Wright**

Are you kidding? I'm always ready for milk and cookies!

**Weisler**

With chocolate chips? Good. I have a couple dozen wonderful stories about how leaders have used milk and cookies to enhance their culture building efforts. Nearly every one of those stories was inspired by the following story.

It was just something I accidentally did right one day as a fairly young supervisor. Our company was growing quickly—from two employees to a thousand in less than two years. As the second person hired, I was privileged to be along for a wonderful, challenging, highly educational ride. As our headcount pushed passed 600, I became aware that we hadn't taken the time lately to pull the troops together and have some meaningful connection.

We were already a fun company and there was nothing identifiably wrong, but I just felt the need to really connect and check in with the people in a way we hadn't really been doing lately. Morale was good. People liked each other. There was no real dissention in the ranks, and in the area of retention and recruitment we were leaders in our industry.

Still, I had the feeling that we needed to do something fun—something that would create a special memory for every employee, something that would give each of them a story to tell; not just a story, but a very fun happy ending type of story. An idea involving milk and cookies came to mind, so I scheduled the CEO for a four-hour meeting that read in his appointment schedule: "Urgent meeting. Subject: Milk and Cookies."

**Wright**
What was his reaction when he saw that on his calendar?

**Weisler**
He called me immediately. "Hey, Kirk, I see you've got me signed out for most of next Tuesday. What am I going to be doing?"

"Don't worry," I said. "Trust me. It will be great." Somehow, I really believed it would be.

I made arrangements with a local bakery for extra-large freshly baked chocolate chip cookies to be delivered in batches of 200 every two hours all day on the next Tuesday. I also contacted the local dairy and found out where I could get those little kindergarten sized milk carton drinks, the kind that we had when we had milk and cookie time when we were in kindergarten.

When my CEO came in on Tuesday morning, I had a cart loaded with still warm, freshly baked cookies and a couple of cases of cold milk. I threw on some napkins for good measure.

For an extra touch of home—and mostly to have fun—I dressed our oh-so-macho CEO in a pink, frilly apron.

He grimaced, then grinned and said, "Okay. Now that you've dressed me like my mother, what's my mission?"

"Your mission," I said, "is to go out there and share the love. Our people are out there on the phones trying to provide great customer service for the companies who hired us to do that, and to be a delight to everyone who calls us.

"Your mission is simply to go out there, show our people that you know they are there, and have fun as you connect with them. You will do that by giving each of them some of these big warm chocolate chip cookies, a couple of cartons of milk, and a big smile—and let them 'feel the love'!"

He smiled and said, "If this is about helping our people feel the love, I'd better start with our chief financial officer because I'm guessing you haven't yet told him he was paying for these cookies."

Then, decked out in a pink, frilly apron, and pushing a cart of warm cookies and cold milk, he headed down the executive hallway to our most grumpy person—our CFO and Controller who, in fact, didn't know that he would soon be getting a bill for well over a thousand cookies.

As I said, there was no real plan for all this. At the time I didn't understand the powerful potential of this exercise; but the results were really exciting. I wish I could tell you that I had planned very deliberately and executed it brilliantly and that I had known great and miraculous things would happen as a result of my incredible brilliance. But that wasn't the case. Of course I hoped something good would happen—I guess all leaders hope for that—but what happened far exceeded my expectations.

The CEO went out there and began to pass these cookies out to our employees, mostly young adults—technicians. I figured he would last a few hours at best, and then I would have someone take over for the evening shift. But I was wrong. Our CEO would not give up that cookie cart to save the world. You couldn't get it away from him. He was having so much fun. He delivered cookies and milk all day, and stayed for the night shift as well. He got engaged. The more engaged he got in this activity of visiting and serving and touching the hearts of his people—well, it was just contagious.

Our already good company morale shot through the ceiling. Our already fun place to work became a warmer and friendlier and an even more fun place to work. But there were other really cool results of "Milk & Cookie Day." Applicants waiting for an open position went from 30 to 300. At the same time that our competitors and peers were actually complaining to the Governor of our state about their diffi-culty in finding qualified people, we had hundreds of qualified appli-cants waiting for an opening.

Our next four or five hiring groups were standing room only. Re-member, we were in the outsource call center/customer service pro-fession. Companies in this industry are not usually considered em-ployers of choice and turnover is typically pretty severe. But our com-pany was considered a great employer, and with Milk & Cookie Day our social capital in the community went up even more.

One of the things we did during new employee orientation was to ask how the new hires had heard about our company. More than half of them said they'd heard about Milk & Cookie Day and thought this would be a really cool company to work for. This little milk and cookie exercise turned out to be a huge recruiting tool, saving us tens of thousands of dollars in recruitment and retraining costs our competi-tors were required to spend because they would never do anything as elementary as buy everyone milk and cookies.

I was brilliant and I didn't even know it. How would I have known that this simple idea—that touched every soul in our company, that cost less than one-half the expenditure of replacing one employee lost to poor culture—would cause such an immediate, positive cultural reaction?

It proved how doing something as simple as giving your people chocolate chip cookies could so easily and "sweetly" shift your culture. It also spoke to that other principle I mentioned earlier, that principle I now teach cultural leaders. Leaders who desire to shift their culture need to give their people a story to tell—a "viral" message that will live a life of its own and spread like wildfire.

When our employees went home after Milk & Cookie Day (which, by the way, they insisted on having again and again every few months), they'd tell their friends that their CEO brings them milk and cookies. These friends would tell their friends and this story is still told nearly seven years later.

Milk & Cookie Day gave them a story to tell and helped them feel more emotionally connected to our company and our company's mis-sion of providing great customer service.

### Wright

This is an easy thing to do—it seems so simple. It seems pretty straightforward. Is there anything to watch out for?

**Weisler**

Sadly enough there is. It seems that no matter how simple or obvious the point, someone with the wrong attitude and approach can, and usually will, mess it up. There are some leaders of organizations who reported to me that they tried it and it was a total flop. When I asked for details I found that they missed the point entirely because they thought it was about the cookies, not the connection. Consequently, they ordered in a huge batch of cookies and several gallons of milk, plopped them down in a central location, and sent around an e-mail saying, "Come and get it." Good grief!

**Wright**

Yes, this idea works because of the principles of service and connection—a hands-on connection. This is something that is pretty rare even in small organizations. When you do it with the right attitude and spirit, and when you combine that with the element of surprise and a pink frilly apron, you also give your people a story to tell that will be told and retold like positive gossip you can never stop—not that you would ever want to.

**Weisler**

That's right. Think about it. Every day, when someone goes home from work or a conference or a meeting, someone—roommate, spouse, friend—is going to ask, "How was work today?" You know that each one of the people you work with is going to tell some kind of story. It might be just a terse "same ol' same ol'"—but if something unique happened (good or bad) they will tell that story—good or bad!

Cultural leaders give them a great response—something fun and interesting to say—a great story to tell. And the story they tell sets the tone and spirit for tomorrow.

**Wright**

That is really interesting. Creating a story like Milk & Cookie Day, that gets retold because it is so unique and also pre-sets the mood for the next day, is simple and inexpensive—yet profitable and fun. Wow.

**Weisler**

Our lives follow our language. What we say today we will get more of tomorrow. There is nothing new about that, but I began to learn that this principle was one you could intentionally harness and utilize as an effective cultural leader. So now I teach cultural leaders to understand that their people are going to be asked a question today— "how did it go at work?" They will either grunt and shrug or they will tell a story (actually a grunt and a shrug is a story, a not-so-good story, but they will tell a story), and if you don't give them a good one to tell, their story will probably sound like a war story or a horror story or just a slice of juicy but negative gossip, and you will have lost your opportunity for some incredibly powerful and positive press.

There are too many people out there telling war stories and exaggerating or horriblizing the day because their circle of friends is doing the same and they don't want to feel left out. So, since we know they are going to tell stories anyway, why not give them a great story to tell? Give them a story that says, "I work for a cool place. You ought to come and work with me."

One of the common themes inherent in the hundred best companies to work for in America is that when you ask an employee of one of these companies how work went on any specific day, they will say odd things like "glorious" and "wonderful." They also say strange things about their company like, "What a great place to work."

To the uninspired, these people are oddballs. They love what they do and they love how they get to do it. They love the people they work with and for, and they love the culture in which they get to work. What they've "got" to do they "get" to do, they are delighted to do it, and those are the stories they tell.

Their friends say, "Gosh, I wish I worked for your company," and that begins to perpetuate a sense of pride that employees get to work somewhere other people want to work. Cultural leaders can create this kind of positive press in a very simple way—give them some warm cookies to eat and a cool story to tell.

### Wright

Wow. This is great. The idea of intentionally creating a moment that gives our people a story to tell can be accomplished with every activity you gave us. If someone read Dr. Seuss to me at work, I would surely go home and tell everyone about it. If someone let me know that I mattered to my company by writing me a "love note" all my friends and family would soon know about it.

### Weisler

These ideas have worked again and again for hundreds of people who, on their journey of improving their workplace cultures, have now blessed tens of thousands of lives. Each idea easily adapts itself to the personality of the person delivering the service, and each idea is personally and culturally rewarding.

**Wright**

Kirk, I know you have to get going and that's too bad. I wish we had time to discuss the rest of your top ten list of ways to create outrageously cool company cultures. What I like is that they aren't complicated theories, just simple, fun, inexpensive little things that make a big difference.

**Weisler**

Most leaders don't want more leadership theory, they want action. They want insights, ideas, and activities that they can do, right now, to make a positive difference. Thank you, David, for our interview today; I've enjoyed our time together.

**Wright**

Me too Kirk, thank you for a fun and insightful experience and for some things I will be doing this week with and for the people I work with here at Insight Publishing.

We've been talking today with Chief Morale Officer Kirk Weisler who travels around the world giving experiential keynotes revealing *everyday* things leaders can do to build great company cultures. Kirk's unique background as a U.S. Army Ranger, his work with at-risk youth, and experience as a master storyteller and team-builder make him a fun, engaging, sought-after speaker.

He is the author of the best smelling book, *The Dog Poop Initiative,* which we have all read here at Insight, and we love it! In addition he has authored *The Cookie Thief, A Question-Able Culture*, and *A More Question-Able Culture.* He is a way out-of-the-box thinker, a make-it-happen guy.

Kirk, thank you again for being with us today on, *Speaking on Success.*

**Weisler**

My pleasure David, and to your readers I say, "Make it a great day. It's your choice!"

# About the Author

In the low morale, high turnover world of outsource call centers with their churn and burn approach to management (creating 150–200 percent annual attrition—and astronomical related costs), a certain reasonably young man created his own title and began his own cultural revolution believing that "work—all work—matters."

While there he developed a full-scale corporate university with a full two-year curriculum, was a prime mover in the creation of over 700 jobs, created an award-winning customer service process, and created an industry-leading employee recognition program. His role as Chief Morale Officer (CMO) helped establish an attrition rate five times less than the industry norm and a 97 percent referral rate for new hires.

Since that day Kirk has been continually invited to share his evangelical cultural-changing message to audiences around the world encouraging, inspiring, and inviting them to create the culture they desire, to take ownership of their environment, and to stop having "a job" and start having a life! He is an expert on creating culture, change, community, and connections in the workplace. Considering how vital the culture issue is to our world of work today, Kirk's message is one that organizations seeking higher levels of employee involvement, engagements, and commitment want and need to hear. His passionate and evangelical delivery on Culture Building and Creating Community are needed more now than at any time in the history of corporate America.

Kirk lives in Atlanta, Georgia, with his, "Wonderful wife, Rebecca, and their five remarkable children who seem to have a fun way of showing up in nearly every presentation he does!"

**Kirk Weisler, Chief Morale Officer**
Team Dynamics, Inc.
100 Olivia Court, Suite 007
Fayetteville, GA 30215
Phone: 404.783.5661
E-mail: kirk@kirkweisler.com
kirkweisler.com
dogpoopinitiative.com
bowlingballonarope.com
givingpeopleastorytotell.com
morebetterbooks.com

# Chapter 7

## Chad Hymas

**David Wright (Wright)**

They say that hindsight is 20/20. With 20/20 hindsight we can look back and see exactly what we did wrong and what happened because of it. We can then accurately kick ourselves for all the things we did wrong.

With 20/20 hindsight we can see clearly what we should or shouldn't have done, and what we wished we had done right. But why can't we see forward as well as we can see backward? Why can't we have 20/20 foresight?

Chad Hymas says we can. At the age of twenty-seven, an accident that he could have prevented changed his life in an instant. The accident happened because Chad was in a hurry and didn't take a few minutes to do something he should have done. He would like to kick himself for not doing what he should have done; but he can't kick himself—he can't kick anything—because he is now paralyzed.

But he doesn't need to kick himself anyway. In the very few years following his accident, Chad has been recognized by the state of Utah as the *Superior Civilian of the Year*. A member of the National

Speakers Association, he travels 150,000 miles a year speaking to hundreds of professional and civic organizations. He is author of a regionally best-selling book, *Soaring to New Heights.*

Chad is a world-class wheelchair athlete—basketball, rugby, hang-gliding, and snow skiing. In July 2003, Chad set a world record by wheeling a 513-mile marathon from Salt Lake City, Utah, to Las Vegas, Nevada.

More important than any of those achievements, Chad and his wife, Shondell, are the proud parents of three children. They reside in Rush Valley, Utah, on a beautiful 5,100-acre private wildlife preserve.

Chad is many more times successful and happy since his "tragic" accident than he was before. Why? It's because of his focus. What is his focus? His focus is *Vision.* He calls it 20/20 vision. Not just 20/20 hindsight, but 20/20 foresight. As a professional speaker, Leadership, Teambuilding, Customer Service, and Mastering Change are his topics, but his focus is 20/20 foresight.

Chad, welcome to *Speaking of Success.*

Tell us more about this thing you call 20/20 foresight or vision and how you came up with that concept.

### Chad Hymas (Hymas)

I was twenty-seven years old in the prime of my life. Everything I had ever desired was coming to me. Life couldn't have been better. I was hurrying to feed the elk on my ranch when the bucket of a tractor with which I was transporting a 2,000-pound bale of hay jerked spasmodically. It flipped the bale backwards and it crashed down on top of me.

I sat there with my neck shattered, my face forced into the steering wheel, totally paralyzed, fighting for my every breath, wondering what was next—if anything.

I wondered if anyone would find me. I wondered if I would be alive when they did. I also wondered how long it would have taken me to add the hydraulic fluid that would have prevented the accident in the first place!

During the time I lay pinned against the steering wheel, and throughout the following sixty-three days I spent in the hospital, I had a lot of time to figure it out. I calculated it would have taken me five to seven minutes to add the hydraulic fluid that would have prevented the accident.

Sure saved a lot of time, didn't I? It now takes me that long to put on one sock! Hindsight—ain't it great? They say hindsight is 20/20. I guess they are right.

My wife found me forty-eight minutes after the bale landed on me. I was air-lifted to LDS Hospital in Salt Lake City. As I lay in the hospital room alone in the dark, berating myself for the mistake that had caused my own accident, my dad came to my bedside and whispered something that changed my perspective—and my life.

He said, "Chad, it's not those who never make mistakes in this life who get ahead, it's those who do fail, accept it, and move on. In fact, son, the most successful are those who fail faster, accept it quicker, then get on with the next step sooner."

What was my next step? I wondered what it would look like since the one thing I couldn't do was "step." I was paralyzed, remember? My next step would be unlike any other I had ever taken. What would it look like? What would my life look like? Would I still have my family? Could I still be a dad? A husband? Well, of course I could. I would be back. I was going to get all better. I was going to walk again. I would be back! I would play ball, referee, run my ranch, and manage my landscaping business. I would be back! I could see it.

### Wright
Tell our readers what it really takes to come back.

### Hymas
Well, actually I was wrong about coming back. What I didn't realize was that I could never come back—I could only come forward. To do that was going to require something new—it was going to require 20/20 foresight—a special kind of vision. This vision would not only draw me forward into an incredible life but also draw forward those who looked to me for leadership—my family, my employees, and now my audiences.

Please, again, do not think I am speaking from ego. I am incredibly blessed, but so can every single person out there be blessed in the same or similar way if each of them will see as I see, with 20/20 vision—20/20 foresight—see clearly what they desire, and let that vision pull them into a beautiful future.

**Wright**

This could not have been easy, especially for a quadriplegic. But you imply that you have a simple formula that anyone can use to move ahead.

**Hymas**

I'm not trying to be clever or cute when I say, "I didn't come back—I went forward." Moving forward doesn't happen overnight, especially when dealing with what appears to be a disaster. It takes seconds for the change to happen, and months, sometimes years, to deal with it and move ahead.

And you don't get over it, you get on with it. That may sound philosophical, and it is. When your body is gone, philosophy, attitude, and vision, are almost all you have left. I say almost—I actually had a lot.

**Wright**

What was it that you had?

**Hymas**

Six years ago I was just like you. I was active physically, played on a basketball team, and had been married for six years to a very beautiful woman. We had two small boys—Christian, three and Kyler, one.

April 2, 2001, sticks out because my wife and I had had an argument. As we reflect back on some of the things we took for granted, we remember that day and how happy we are that we were quick to make up that evening, because the very next day was a changing day for both of us.

One night I was happily making up with my wife from an argument—my fault I'm sure—three nights later I woke up in the hospital, from the accident, not from the argument!

I was in a halo, a contraption that is not angelic by any means. It is a brace—a metal ring around your head, hooked up to weights and screwed right through your skin into your skull. It hurts like crazy and it doesn't allow you to move—not a fraction of an inch.

As I awoke, there were two doctors standing in front of me. My wife was on my left stroking my hand. I couldn't feel it at all. My mother and father were on my right as I was told bluntly that I was a quadriplegic.

Can you imagine waking up and trying to look down to see where your body went? It is eerie, spooky, and horribly unsettling to say the least.

I struggled against it, but how do you struggle with a body that won't struggle or respond in any way? There was no movement at that time—none.

The doctors did give me some good news. They said, "Hey, Chad, good news. We think you're going to get one wrist back and a shoulder and you might have some use of one arm but definitely not all of it. Other than that, you won't have any feeling in your body from the breast line down."

Good news? I wondered what "bad news" might sound like. Oh yeah, it would sound like this: "Hi, I'm St. Peter . . ."

Day sixty-three was pivotal for me. I had been sixty-two days in the hospital going numbly—literally—through rehabilitation. I went through the motions, unable to see what my future held; but being warehoused with nothing but steel and plastic keeping me alive sure as heck wasn't going to be it. Day sixty-three was also the day I met Art Berg. Or, rather, he met me.

**Wright**

Art Berg the speaker, I assume.

**Hymas**

Yes, also Art Berg the author, Art Berg the business owner, and Art Berg the wheelchair athlete. Art was also a quadriplegic. He's very, very well known in the speaking world. Of course I had no idea who he was. I was a farmer. I was an elk breeder. To me, Art was just another guy in a wheelchair whose hands didn't work so well—like mine.

He wheels his chair into my hospital room. Without a word, he throws himself onto my bed and takes off his clothes. That was quite a shock, but I was in no shape to run away. Then he puts them back on faster with the use of hardly anything more than most people do with the use of everything.

He then flings himself off the bed and back onto his wheelchair, looks up at me and grins. Finally he tells me his name, pulls a book out, signs it, and puts it on my bed. He had no better grip than I did, but he obviously had gotten a better grip on life than I had. I noticed the title, *Some Miracles Take Time*. The subtitle was, *The difficult takes time; the impossible just takes a little longer.*

He told me to call him sometime, then wheeled out the door just as he had wheeled in—leaving me speechless. My wife says that was the last time I was ever speechless.

So I called him. I didn't call him because I wanted to become a speaker, I called him because I wanted to get back to landscaping and ranching. I needed to ask him how to get through all this. How do you use the bathroom? How do I court my wife? How do I stay married? How do I get back to my life? He said, "You don't go back, Chad. You go forward."

I didn't pay attention. I didn't need cute philosophy, I needed answers. How do I show my kids how to jump off the left foot and shoot with the right hand in basketball? How do I mow my lawn? How do I make love to my wife? That was important to me and I know it is important to a lot of folks out there who are paralyzed like me—and who are paralyzed in a lot of other ways.

Art was a busy man—a professional speaker—one of the greats in the National Speakers Association. And here he was teaching me really personal stuff.

I asked him how he drove. He took me out and showed me. He showed me how to catheterize myself so I could go to the bathroom without assistance. He showed me how to ride a bike, shoot a gun, and discipline my kids from a wheelchair. He didn't just tell me, he took the time and showed me.

Art was married to a very, very beautiful woman, Dallas. I thought, "I am married to a beautiful woman and have two great kids. Art is married to a beautiful woman and has two great kids. My friend Mike Schlappi, also a wheelchair-bound national speaker, is married to a beautiful woman and they have a great family too—hey, maybe there are compensations in life."

I also learned that Art spoke professionally—and was paid very well for it. I thought this was pretty crazy. I didn't know that one could make a living just talking.

**Wright**

Well, you are making a good living at it.

**Hymas**

Yes, but that wasn't my plan. I just wanted to live a normal life.

One of the things I missed most was competition. I learned that Art set a world record back in 1993 going 325 miles—from Salt Lake

City to St. George—in his wheelchair. Could I do something like that? Just to prove to myself I could?

Art invited Shondell and me to go to Honolulu, Hawaii, with him to listen to him speak, so we did. Shondell and I decided to make it a second honeymoon, so we left our children at home and we went to a luxury hotel right on the beach, the Honolulu Marriott.

No, Shondell did not carry me over the threshold (give me a break). She sat on my lap and I wheeled her over in style!

We watched Art speak that night, and I was amazed that he spoke simply and powerfully from what most would call a weak position—that of a wheelchair-bound quadriplegic.

Afterward, he told me I could speak too. "Chad, be your own artist. Color your own picture and share it with the world." I think he was telling me not to steal his stuff! Those were the last words he ever spoke to me.

### Wright

Why? What happened?

### Hymas

We returned home on February 19, 2002. Five days later Art Berg died. He passed away in his sleep. Nobody was affected by that more than I was. I say that selfishly. I'm sure his family suffered more—but I was devastated.

I forced my way past my wife—I am always so sensitive—and pushed my chair down the asphalt country road for miles wondering what it was all about. Why didn't I just take the time to put one lousy quart of hydraulic fluid in that darn hoist? Hindsight sure is 20/20, isn't it?

As I pushed down the road, I did not realize I had just begun the training that would eventually lead to breaking Art's wheelchair record. How was I going to make it without Art? Who could fill his shoes (or rather, his chair)? He wasn't just a mentor to me to be a speaker, but to be a contributing "normal" human being, husband, father—man. I had lost my guide who was just starting to help me through this overwhelming maze of adjustment. However, maybe he had already given me what I needed.

As I headed for home, after having gone much farther than I should have, I grew weary. But I noticed how much easier it was if I looked up—if I focused on where I was headed. It sure didn't matter what was behind me. What is that scripture in Luke? "No man, having put his hand to the plow and looking back is fit for the king-dom . . ." (Luke 9:62).

What is behind is only as important as what can be learned from it. Use that 20/20 hindsight to see the truth clearly. Then let the past go and use what you learn to move ahead. Focus on your vision and let its power move you ahead. I focused on the lights of my home and found it much easier to get there, though I was weary to the bone.

Art hadn't left me stranded after all. He had given me exactly what I needed—he taught me the power of clear vision, the power of 20/20 foresight. I could see something now ahead of me.

**Wright**

What did you see?

**Hymas**

A simple, clear goal. I was out there one day thinking about what to do next, pushing my wheelchair along with the heels of my para-lyzed hands, and I felt impressed to see if I could beat my mentor's world record.

I trained for eighteen months. I pushed from Salt Lake City to Las Vegas. I did set a new world record. Now, the details involved heat and sweat and pain, but the essence was that I had a vision, kept my eyes on the goal, I didn't look back (except when I wanted to quit and my wife wouldn't let me), and I (we) won the prize—the trophy. My wife claims the trophy—she says that if it wasn't for her I would have given up. She is right, so now I call her my trophy wife.

Why did I go after a world record? Because—well—because I wanted to. I didn't realize it would lead to something, I just wanted to do it and so I did. And, after that, things started to happen.

**Wright**

What happened?

**Hymas**

Following the news coverage of my trek to Las Vegas, I was asked to speak at a big convention. I hesitated. What did I have to say to a bunch of able-bodied, successful corporate men and women? Then I remembered how powerful Art was when he simply told his story—just being real and having fun.

I gave my speech. I tried to be real. I had fun and I fell in love with it. I made some national talk shows and I've been speaking professionally ever since. That first year I had seven speaking engagements. This last year we had 193. That's the short of the long story. It sounds easy but it wasn't. There is no way to move down the road quickly or easily—even with smooth asphalt and rubber tires.

Today, I am still learning how to get along. I travel by myself. I found that the more I depend on other people the more independent I become. Most people don't ever learn that. Some CEOs never learn that. I am independent, but I depend on others for help getting over a non-accommodating curb or transferring from my wheelchair. I have learned to ask—simply and specifically—for help.

Because I am willing to ask for help, I get to travel all over the world. This is possible because I ask simply and specifically and give positive feedback when others help me. Just like any CEO, if my people don't do it right I will get dropped on my head and that hurts!

I have learned that there are caring strangers all around who never saw me before and will probably never see me again but who are happy to help if I just ask. Some are strangers who don't even speak my language; instead, they speak the common language of caring humanity.

I have learned that it is the gift of clear vision and 20/20 foresight that gets the job done. I know exactly what I want and, because I can see it clearly, my instructions and requests are clear and precise. Even strangers who struggle with English get my intent clearly and I get to where I want to go safely and efficiently.

People are very giving if you are willing to depend on them. I found that the more I am willing to admit my dependence on others the more independent and powerful I become.

**Wright**

How does becoming dependent on others empower us?

**Hymas**

Not becoming dependent—admitting that we already are. What would happen if we would admit to our spouses and our kids that we depend on them? What if CEOs were willing to admit their dependence on their staff? What if they shared their vision and then simply and humbly asked their people to help them achieve it?

**Wright**

Maybe their people would pull together better?

**Hymas**

Right. And maybe the CEO wouldn't have to be there every single day and would have time to go on a vacation or spend time with the family or play golf or take sixty-three days off after dropping a two-ton bale of hay on his head. Better yet, maybe he or she would have time to do the simple but important things like adding a can of hydraulic fluid when it is needed and prevent the disaster in the first place.

**Wright**

Chad, you seem to know a lot of things about management that aren't in the textbooks. What characteristics have you observed in people who are most successful at getting their team to help them get what they want?

**Hymas**

They are men and women of vision—not just grandiose vision, though that larger vision is important. In his book, *Good to Great,* Jim Collins calls it a "Big Hairy Audacious Goal." They also see what needs to be done right now, today, and tomorrow. They let the energy of that vision move them through any problem, even if the solution isn't readily apparent.

**Wright**

Well, that makes sense. If the solution is obvious, who needs vision—or leaders for that matter?

**Hymas**

Right. Leaders have vision. They have 20/20 foresight. They see the future as clearly as others see the past. They learn from the past, but their focus is on the future—where they are headed, not where they've been.

Twenty-twenty foresight is a common trait among successful people. They see very clearly what hasn't happened yet but intend it to—and it does. They stay focused on the destination. They put their hand to the plow, they don't look back, and they reap the harvest.

**Wright**

Chad, you went through a lot of tedious, repetitive work just to relearn how to do the simplest things. Isn't that boring? What do you do when it gets boring and tedious?

**Hymas**

The road to success is paved with small and sometimes tedious and boring steps. Do you know how many yellow stripes there are between Mesquite and Los Vegas, Nevada? There are 6,752. I counted 'em on my record-breaking journey. That is tedium, but if what you do makes the vision of what you desire real, then you do what you have to do to succeed. Remember the Code of the West? "A man's gotta do what a man's gotta do." But we don't always do it. Why? 'Cause it's no fun. So, tedious or not, I say it like this, "I do what I gotta do, so I get what I wanna get."

**Wright**

Attaching tough work today to a great reward later, that's what you get to do, even if it is tedious?

**Hymas**

Exactly. Every successful leader I know of was clear about what he or she wanted and why, and was willing to do a lot of difficult, even tedious work to get there. These leaders approached even tedium with a certain degree of enthusiasm because they saw the direct connection to getting what they desired. Successful people are constantly focused on the prize with 20/20 foresight, and they let the thrill of that vision give them the energy to do what is necessary to get there.

After meeting Art Berg, I realized that I wasn't going to walk in a few weeks or maybe even a few years. But that did not mean that I couldn't achieve everything I wanted. I just had to see it differently. Successful leaders are willing to accept changing circumstances, yet keep their foresight 20/20.

The world of today is constantly changing. Technology is a great example. You have to be willing to relearn—even start all over again—just to keep from becoming a dinosaur.

Microsoft came out with a new version. My editor has it and so I'd better get it because the old version isn't good enough for what I want to accomplish. Twenty-twenty foresight helps you accept new circumstances and conditions without changing your vision.

On April 2nd I was just fine. On April 3rd a two-ton bale of hay altered my circumstances and I had to accept new facts and conditions. I had to relearn practically everything, starting with the simple things. I desire to live in normal society and eat at great restaurants with my wife or with clients; so what do I need to do to eat so I don't get food all over the people sitting next to me? What technology exists to help me? What do I have to learn or maybe invent so I can use utensils without assistance and without making a mess and splattering food all over? Am I willing to do that?

How can I drive without using my feet or hands? Can I use my wrists? Am I willing to learn to do that? How can I run my business? How can I be a husband? Not just a provider, but a real husband? This is very, very personal and I don't mind sharing it with you. The toughest thing that I've ever done in my life by far is to relearn how to be romantic with my wife. Face it. Considering a twenty-seven-year-old kid's ego, romantic intimacy is pretty important in his marriage.

So how did I deal with it? How did I save my marriage? I didn't. I was too thick-headed and wrapped up in my ego. It was my wife who saved my marriage. Well, I did do one thing right—I shut up and listened to her when she came to me and said, "Chad, you think you can't meet my needs—but you are wrong." I am a man. I am used to being wrong, so I kept listening. "You think my needs are the same as yours. They aren't. Men's needs are different than women's. Men really are from Mars and we women really do live on another planet—especially when it comes to love and romance."

My incredible, loving wife cut right through my thick-headed ego and changed the way I believe. My Shondell stuck it out when I was really tough to deal with. Because of her, more than because of me, we'll celebrate our twelfth anniversary this March.

For more than half of those years I've been in a wheelchair and during that half we have lived and loved better than the first half; all because of what my wife helped me learn about our relationship. She saved our marriage. I will forever love and respect her immensely for that. I take credit only for being smart enough to listen to her.

In my vision for the future, Shondell and I have a little girl. I am a quad. How do we produce a little girl? Well, I don't know, exactly, but I know we will if we focus on the vision of a bright beautiful little girl playing in a ray of sunlight on our carpet in our home, looking up and calling me "Daddy," then let the thrill of that vision pull us to it.

We did just that and solutions continued to come to us. We looked ahead with 20/20 foresight and let that vision work in us. It drove our creative engine and "voila!" we have a miracle. Through the miracle of modern science or adoption—or of a loving God—my Shondell and I saw with perfect foresight our little girl in our future. And now here she is in our present—our little girl from Guatemala—our little Gracee.

Dreams are coming true in my life—our life—because I am willing to focus on a vision of my own creation and have faith that the details will work themselves out.

Successful people, other CEOs, and other business and community leaders deal effectively with change by looking ahead with 20/20 foresight and seeing what they desire—clearly and in detail—they let their vision pull them forward. In my case and in Mike Schlappi's and Art Berg's situation, we let the power of that vision, *roll* us forward. This is the key ingredient in the formula for success.

**Wright**

I guess you have answered this already, but let me ask it anyway. Would these things that you have learned also apply to people who are not in wheelchairs?

**Hymas**

Definitely. Everyone has some sort of challenge. Mine is visible. Others' challenges may be invisible, but just as crippling. Someone has lost a loved one or someone's teenager makes a bad decision or someone is going through divorce or dealing with a dying parent. Someone is dealing with changes in the workplace. It can leave you feeling helpless—not knowing what to do next and, therefore, not doing anything. That is just as paralyzing as breaking your neck.

Paralysis is overcome more by vision and faith than by any other single thing. Look ahead with foresight and see with 20/20 foresight. Then exercise the faith to let that vision pull you forward.

My friend and fellow speaker, Kate Adamson, put it beautifully: "We focus on what we want, not on what we don't; on what we have not on what we don't; and what we can do, not on what we can't." It is that vision that pulls us into a wonderful future of our own creation.

By the way, Kate was more paralyzed than a quadriplegic. What can be more paralyzed than a quad? She was 100 percent paralyzed. Except for a stubborn heart that kept beating, Kate could do nothing. She could not move a finger or a toe. She communicated by blinking her eyes in a special code. Now she is a professional speaker and author just like me but she is better looking!

Kate could never have made it back—I mean forward—without focusing with 20/20 foresight—on her vision—not on her past injury and the unfairness of it. She is alive and inspiring others today because of it.

I might be paralyzed physically; others are paralyzed financially, technologically, emotionally, or mentally. Mike Schlappi was paralyzed by a bullet. My friend, Greg, was paralyzed by clinical depression, my editor is visually impaired by his DNA; but they all keep moving forward speaking and writing and accomplishing wonderful things by keeping their focus on their vision with 20/20 foresight.

Paralysis comes in many, many forms. How to deal with non-physical paralysis is no different from dealing with physical paralysis. I have lost 90 percent of my feeling and muscle control in my body.

Others have lost other things just as important—jobs, loved ones, financial security. How do they get through it? They visualize what they desire and focus on what they have, not what they have lost. They keep that vision in front of them and let that pull them through—like lassoing a shooting star.

During hurricane Katrina, 173 people stood on the rooftops of their homes that were covered in water. They refused to get on the rescue helicopters. According to some reports they actually shot at the helicopters! Now there were several hundred others who left their homes and were rescued. But 173 people stood there with guns in their hands refusing to leave their soggy possessions. What was our government's choice? They couldn't be forced—not when they were armed and dangerous—so they had to be left behind.

Those 173 people died. That's a fact. I don't want to offend anybody so I don't always share this with audiences, but that's the truth. Is that a fair price to pay for hanging on to what is already gone? Is it worth your life to not get what you can from your 20/20 hindsight and then get on with life with 20/20 foresight?

In a way, I had that same choice. Is it worth my life and my marriage and my kids for me to not change and maybe even die because I didn't want to change? No. "I gotta do what I gotta do so I will get to "have what I wanna have!"

### Wright

Do you agree with most behavioral scientists that dealing with change by letting go of the past and moving forward with 20/20 vision is the most difficult thing human beings ever do?

### Hymas

I don't know if it's the most difficult, but it is the most important. It can be difficult. It was for me. Many times I wanted to give up.

Then I would visualize my goal and that gave me the energy for the next step and the next, etc.

I still have bad days. Sometimes I look outside and see my kids playing ball and yearn to play with them. I admit I feel sad about what I have lost. Heck, I played college basketball. I love hoops and of course I want to play.

So I do. I roll out there in my chair and do what I can do. What can I do? Help my kids learn to keep their focus on the goal. I tell them to see what they want, not what they don't want. I teach them to focus on the basket and see the ball go where they want it to go. That is a perfect example of 20/20 foresight. The better their focus on the goal, the more consistently they score. Anyone who has played ball knows this. Does it work in business as well? In family life? It does.

**Wright**

So you not only get to play ball with your kids, you actually can coach them?

**Hymas**

That's right. I coach from the bench, so to speak. I don't have to show them, I just tell them and they believe me—because I am their dad. Of course that will wear off as soon as they hit their teens, but I can bask in the glory of coaching from the bench for a little while longer.

I could bemoan the fact that I can't play. But I don't focus on what I've lost. I focus on what I have and am grateful to my Creator for it.

Look, here I am in an incredible office, with a seventy-five-gallon exotic fish aquarium. It even has fish in it—and my little fishie friends are really glad that I saw Art Berg grip things with his wrists, and could see myself doing the same; because I can now grip a can of fish food and my little wiggly friends get dinner.

Because I was inspired by a great man to focus on my vision of the future, I have a beautiful home and a wonderful office with auto-graphed pictures and posters all over my wall from motivational speakers and world leaders I have met and who have changed my life.

Would I have all this had I not been hurt? Probably not. One thing for sure is that I wouldn't have my precious little girl—and she is worth it all.

**Wright**

If you could go back and change it would you?

## Chad

No. No, I wouldn't change it. That doesn't mean that I don't want to walk again, I do want to. Because of the unique characteristics of my injury I still have significant muscle tone in my legs and I believe that somehow, through the miracle of science or the miracle of a blessing, I will re-establish those nerve connections. I would love to walk again. I would love to have feeling in my body. That's my "Big Goal." And so I will keep focusing on what I desire and let that clear 20/20 vision draw me ever forward.

But what if it doesn't happen? I'm not going to sit around and wait for it. There is too much for me to do today. I've got a daughter who depends on me to read to her. I've got two boys who love basketball and by golly, I can coach them from the bench. Maybe that will be the title of my next book, *Coaching from the Bench.*

I have an awesome life as a direct result of what I have learned and traits I have gained from the accident. I've got a beautiful wife who makes my life joyful and whom I love to make happy. I get to speak to thousands of people, some of whom depend on me as I depended on Art Berg. This week I'll visit three different states. My life is wonderful.

## Wright

Most of the time when people have success like you do, they have a mentor who made the difference. I know that Art Berg had an impact on you because it was such an immediate thing and he had been through such a similar experience; but were there others who made a difference?

## Hymas

Family. I have a great family. I grew up in a Christian home and faith was very important. When I got hurt, Dad quit his job of twenty-two years and took over my dream of being a rancher. That dream is still alive today. My dad kept my dream alive so that I could see it live and my boys could one day inherit it.

My income comes from speaking and writing. The ranch income is my dad's—and he sure earns it. He didn't have to give up his career for me. But he did.

My mother also quit her job to help me through rehab. She is an angel. I can never repay them for giving me my start in life—twice. Can you imagine teaching your son to feed himself—twice? I can never repay them; all I can do is make them proud of me again by moving forward with enthusiasm and vision.

**Wright**
What about your landscaping business?

**Hymas**
Remember what I said earlier about being willing to share the vision and hand over control to others? Well I did that, but not on purpose. It was thrust on me.

For seven years my dream was to plant trees, plant flowers, and grass, put in sprinkler systems, and mow lawns. That's what I did for a living. My brothers helped me build that business. We did it for seven years and I loved it. For a hobby, I raised elk. That's what we did for fun and we made a little profit on the side.

I had thirty-five employees before I broke my neck. When I was in the hospital I had to let every one of those guys go because I thought there was nobody else to run the business. It was my vision, right? Not theirs, right? So I gave each of them a few months' pay and told them that I was grateful for their service and was sorry I had to let them go.

But the rascals didn't go. They had taken over my vision. I had accidentally done something right in the way I had hired and managed my team.

When I arrived at home on day sixty-three all thirty-five of them were standing in my driveway with their families. Then, on cue, they stepped aside revealing a new cement ramp to my front door. Not some piece-of-junk ramp made out of plywood because of some government regulation; this was done right—a ramp built with love and respect.

I wheeled into my house and through tears of gratitude saw that they had built a deck all around my house so I could go out in the fresh air and see my elk any time I wanted to. There is nothing quite like watching baby elk play in the spring or adolescent elk trying out their head-butting skills in the fall to impress the ladies. I know building that deck wasn't cheap—but no matter what it cost it is priceless.

Then they took me back into the house and showed me where they had cut a hole in the floor and installed an elevator so I could get down to my office—and I guess so the kids could play on it because they think that's what it's for.

Finally, they showed me the master bathroom. They had torn out the extra sink and made a roll-in shower for me. I don't know why we needed two sinks anyway. They were both for Shondell—and she only has one face (a pretty one too).

You talk about leadership and successful people—I thought I had to shut the business down and let my employees go. Not only did they refuse to go, but most of them are still here. My landscaping business survived. It is not just my dream, it is theirs. Vision—20/20 foresight. Once mine, now theirs—ours.

**Wright**

Have you gained any specific expertise from this experience?

**Hymas**

Yes. Performance management—managing others by including them in your vision, whether long-range or short-range, thereby enlisting their willing and enthusiastic assistance. When you have to suck up your pride (something quadriplegics have to do all the time) and ask people to do simple things for you, you learn to get people to do simple yet noble things. The results are amazing.

**Wright**

If I had been speaking to you on April 2, 2001, at that stage in your life, what would you have told me your dreams and aspirations for the future would have been?

**Hymas**

I wanted a big family. I wanted to move forward in my coaching and see if I couldn't pursue maybe some collegiate refereeing opportunities. I had big dreams for my landscaping business. I wanted great things for my family.

**Wright**

And then the tragedy . . .

**Hymas**

Well, many people including my own mother said it was a tragedy; and indeed it was, or it seemed to be. But as I look back it wasn't so tragic after all. Change brings opportunity and this accident brought a lot of opportunity with it. Of course I didn't feel that way about it for awhile—and it certainly wasn't apparent.

**Wright**

Well, yes. The opportunity couldn't have been apparent immediately.

**Hymas**

I had shattered three out of seven of the vertebrae in my neck: C-4 C-5, and C-6. That caused me to lose the complete use of my feet, my legs, all my stomach muscles, two out of my three major chest muscles, most of the strength and use of my arms, and I lost the complete use and feeling in my fingers and hands. It sure didn't feel like an "opportunity." Could I still be a husband? Could I still be a father? Could I work?

**Wright**

How did you cope in those early days with that fear? Did you share your fear with others or were you in lonely isolation?

**Hymas**

I was isolated but not really lonely. I was in the hospital for sixty-three days. I was comfortable there because I was around people who were like me and I still had the belief that this wasn't really happening.

I was in all kinds of denial. The doctors told me that a high percentage of people like me lost their spouse within the first couple of months. I wasn't listening.

They didn't tell me I would lose Shondell because she wouldn't love me anymore. My Doctor said, "Chad, you are going to push her away."

I didn't understand what he was saying until I got home and then I found out what they meant.

My life was gone. I could not see tomorrow. I couldn't even see today. I couldn't see myself doing anything good or right or fun. When I dreamed at night, my dreams were always about my happy past—doing normal things as I had done before in a normally functioning body—working, playing ball, playing with my kids, standing hand-in-hand with my wife, Shondell, feeling her touch, watching the baby elk play. Then I would wake up to a body that didn't even exist. I wasn't feeling sorry for myself. I wasn't feeling much of anything. I was numb, emotionally and physically.

I found myself doing what the doctors told me I would be doing. I started pushing my sweetheart away. See, I didn't marry Shondell to watch her mow the lawn, put gas in my car, get me dressed, help me use the restroom. I didn't like watching her do that for me. And I saw myself begin to push her away.

One day Shondell was transferring me from the shower chair to this very wheelchair—and she accidentally dropped me. I looked up at her face from the ground and I saw a bead of sweat slide down her cheek. And that was it. I lost it. I'd had enough. I didn't marry her to watch her labor over me. I let myself believe that I was too much of a man for this and I let myself believe it was humiliating. I verbally kicked her out of the room.

She went out and stood on the other side of the door, quietly crying; but she would not go farther than a few feet away from me. I was too much into my own selfish pain to think about what that had done to her.

The phone rang. It was my mother-in law (of all people). I have a great relationship with Char, my mother-in-law. She asked to talk to me. She could have ripped me apart but she knew I was struggling. She let me explain to her for the next ninety minutes the very things I just told you in thirty seconds—over and over again.

"I didn't marry your daughter to watch her do this," I raved.

Finally she said, "Are you through yet?"

Sarcastically I replied, "Yes."

The second thing she said was, "This is the most selfish person I have ever seen you be, Chad. When you say it wasn't why you married my daughter, apparently you weren't listening to yourself when you made the promises you made on your wedding day."

And the last thing she said hit me like a brick to the face, "Chad, you want to know the greatest thing you can give my daughter?"

"What?" I replied flatly.

"You can give her your most gracious acceptance."

Ouch. I had to be a real man. I had to swallow my stupid pride and recognize her ability to give to me. Recognize what she really wants to do. Recognize her attributes, her skills, her counsel—everything a marriage should entail. Not only recognize it, but thank her for it. So I've tried to do that every day of my life from then on.

**Wright**

Is it hard?

**Hymas**

Yes it is difficult. Why? Not pride—lack of vision. Not looking with 20/20 foresight at how our life would look if I would let my wife be who she really is—my partner, my equal. But when I do and she does, wow! They say hindsight is 20/20. I say foresight—vision—is 20/20 because we create exactly what we see.

**Wright**

So that's the turning point? You caught the vision of what a real partnership would be?

**Hymas**

That's right; thanks to my mother-in-law.

**Wright**

Chad, is there anyone in your life who somehow prepared you for this, or taught you something that now you're able to use?

**Hymas**

I am where I am today mostly because of my family; but I often find myself thinking about a very special individual who helped prepare me for this day with the help of my dad. Her name is Melanie.

I was a "jock" in high school. I was cool. I don't think I was mean, but as high school athletes often do, I thought I was "all that." At lunch I sat in the cafeteria with my basketball buddies. At the middle table sat the Special Ed' kids—many in wheelchairs.

One of them was a girl named Melanie. When she ate, her food ended up on her shirt, on her lap, on the floor. She used a computer to talk. She often drooled.

I am ashamed to admit it, but for whatever reason my friends and I thought that was kinda funny. One day after basketball practice we were all at my house—downstairs in my room—laughing and joking about Melanie. There comes a knock at my bedroom door.

It was my dad—he had been standing on the other side of the door and had heard everything we had said.

He came in and sat down on the bed. He sat quietly for a moment and then quietly but firmly set us straight.

"Do you want Melanie to have a life filled with loneliness or filled with good friends?" He asked.

We mumbled whatever we could mumble with our feet in our mouths. Then Dad left the room. But he wasn't done with us yet.

The next day at school he cinched it. I was sitting with my buddies. Melanie was sitting at the Special Ed' table. My dad walked into the cafeteria and right over to our table. Quietly, he asked, "Chad, where is Melanie sitting?"

"Over there," I replied. "She's the one with the computer on her chair."

"You and your buddies, follow me."

We followed Dad over to her table. He tapped Melanie on her shoulder and said, "Melanie, my name is Kelly Hymas. This is my son, Chad. These are his friends," and he introduced each by name.

Then he asked her, "How would you like to go to McDonald's with us and grab a milkshake?"

She typed on her computer, "I'm sorry, sir; but my mother won't let me go out with strangers."

I thought that was a classic response.

**Wright**

(laughing) Very good.

**Hymas**

So Dad took Melanie to the principal's office. The principal called her mother and received permission from her. My dad then picked Melanie up out of the chair and deposited her on the front passenger seat. We piled into the van.

We went to McDonald's together—ten "jocks" and a girl in a wheelchair in a van that only seats six. And I was able to find out more about her. I also found out more about me.

Melanie became part of the gang. Did we change her life? I hope so, because she sure changed ours. Because she hung out with us, people realized what a wonderful, witty, fun person she really was. Melanie was elected Head Cheerleader.

I think about her every day because today I get to go through just a little bit of what she went through every single day of her life.

**Wright**

Chad, since your accident, has faith played an important role in the decisions you have made?

**Hymas**

I have tried to have more humility and more faith in the last three or four years (I say "in the last three or four years" because it took me a few years to figure it out. Is that okay to say?) But now faith is huge for me.

A vision isn't much good without faith. Or, I don't know, maybe a vision creates faith. Certainly a vision creates desire and desire is the driving force that pulls you ahead. All I know is that vision and faith go hand-in-hand. You can see clearly what you desire—that's vision— then you believe in it because you can see it in detail and that belief or faith moves you closer to the vision and that vision gets clearer and clearer until one day you realize why it is so clear. It is real. She is playing on the carpet in front of you, looking up, and calling you "Daddy."

Art Berg said, "What you see drives your beliefs and that drives your actions and consequently your results." I respectfully add, what you see drives your beliefs and that drives your actions and consequently your results. What do I believe about speaking for a living? What do I have to say? How will I say it? Do I see myself listening to my audience as well? How will that impact and influence them?

Art Berg built me a high platform and told me to move higher from there. And that's why I have the world record trophies I have. I'm not talking about the wheelchair run from Salt Lake to Vegas, which, by the way, I did in Art Berg's chair to honor him. I'm talking about all the other wonderful things I have because I didn't give in to my paralysis. I stayed focused on my vision and let it pull me forward.

Where is my focus, and what do I believe? Since my accident, 20/20 foresight and focus—seeing myself as the father of a little girl— and the blessings of Heaven—gave me my precious little daughter. Seeing myself connect with individuals in an audience of thousands has created my professional speaking business. I can now get dressed in forty-seven minutes; Art could do it twice as fast but I am proud of my accomplishment. I never thought I would do as well as I do.

It took me sixteen months to learn how to drive a car again and the first time out I drove less than one mile, but that is a world record for me—maybe it's a pretty small world, but a trophy win nonetheless. The fact that I was on the front page of the *Wall Street Journal*, that's a world record—for me. Those are trophies—Shondell even calls herself my trophy wife. I agree—you will too when you meet her.

These wonderful things that are happening in my life are things that I never dreamed of. Those are my trophies and they are way beyond anything I would have ever thought I would achieve until Art Berg taught me to look ahead with 20/20 foresight and let that vision drive my faith and my faith drive my actions—even the repetitive tedious practice of learning to shave, brush my teeth, and put on my own socks. And now I get to take my vision to the world.

**Wright**

When you speak, what vision do you want your audience to see?

**Hymas**

I want my audiences to catch the vision of the wonderful life they will live when they stay focused on their vision with 20/20 foresight and faith. They don't have to be religious to see a vision, they just have to be a little imaginative. And when they are, miracles happen.

**Wright**

You are one of those rare individuals who understand your right and obligation to make a difference where you are with what you've got.

As we sit here in this studio, on this particular day, it's only been a few years since the accident and yet you have accomplished so much. You own your own business. You travel around the country speaking to literally thousands of people. You are still actively involved in competitive sports. You are the world record-holder for quadriplegics in cross-country wheelchair. It has taken you a relatively few years to get to the point where you are today.

What have you discovered about yourself that you really don't believe you would have ever discovered had it not been for the accident?

**Hymas**

I learned I had the latent ability to see tomorrow and to act on that vision. I don't say that to say I am all that special. It is just something I was blessed with, I guess. Vision is the catalyst that creates extraordinary results. And I have the power to see what I want to see. I didn't realize I had that power before my accident. I was able to create a vision and let that vision draw me into it.

Today, when I wake up in the morning, I have the power to decide what I want to see. I can choose my vision—my 20/20 foresight. I get to decide what it looks like. I can choose to see it. I let that vision work in my mind, play in it, dream about it, and let that vision pull me into my day.

**Wright**

So, with the answer you just now offered, I hear you saying that this isn't really a special skill or trait—there is no one who couldn't do what you're suggesting.

**Hymas**

That's right. And it is not complicated. I was just average before and I'm still just average today. But all of us "average" folks have great power. We have the power to choose our vision—to choose what we see and how clearly we see it. Some are more naturally inclined, maybe even more easily imaginative, but it is a skill—a mental habit that can be learned by anyone who wants extraordinary results.

We can all see with 20/20 foresight. We can create our own vision and thereby create our own results. We've all been given that ability to choose what we want to see and therefore do with every twenty-four-hour day we are blessed to live. We can choose our future and create our own destiny. Vision is the single most important factor in a successful and joyful life.

Visualization is throwing out a mental grappling hook and pulling yourself toward it. Vision somehow becomes an active force as you hook into it; it also draws you toward itself. Anyone can do this.

Try it right now. Think of something you want to have or do—think of who you want to be. How does it look? Are there colors? How does it taste? Does it have a texture? A sound to it? How does it feel? Is it warm? How does it feel emotionally? Does it involve a happy marriage? A healthy bank account?

See how the more clearly you focus on the vision, enlisting as many senses as possible, creates energy, drive, and desire? Well, that energy and desire also creates solutions, methods, and techniques.

From deep in your subconscious—even from the very soul of you—depending on how important this goal is that you are visualizing, comes power and purpose and desire and drive—and technique and skill—sufficient to get you there.

**Wright**

You said before, when we first started this conversation, that people around you, even your mother saw this accident as a tragedy.

**Hymas**

She wouldn't call it that today.

**Wright**

That's my question.

**Hymas**

Yeah, she wouldn't. She would tell you this has been one of the most significant blessings of my life—one of the most significant blessings of her life.

I am better with my kids. I discipline them differently. My kids are my friends. Do they need discipline? Yes. But Christian is taller than his dad today. Try disciplining your kid from your knees. It is an incredible experience. You can teach 'em better from your knees. Everything's different and, honestly, many things are much better—even things you wouldn't think were.

**Wright**

Wonderful story. How about the future? How you see your life thirty years from today?

**Hymas**

Thirty years from today I see myself happy—still happy; whether I'm walking or not. I see myself happy. I see myself with my boys and my girl. I see myself involved with their families. And, most important, I see myself still married and deeply, romantically in love with my Shondell—the girl of my dreams.

I'll still be telling my stories and hearing others. And telling my story never gets old because it's different every time. Everyone is different and whenever I share it with others I relate to them in different ways.

**Wright**

Will you walk again?

**Hymas**

I have a dream. In my dream I am walking again. I see myself holding Shondell's hand as we walk down the street. I see myself playing ball with my kids. I see myself dancing with my wife again to "our song," "Save the Best for Last," by Vanessa Williams:

> *"Sometimes the snow comes down in June.*
> *Sometimes the sun goes around the moon;*
> *Just when you thought you were falling fast,*
> *You go and save the best for last."*

I'd say that was prophetic. But I'm not going to wait for that to happen. I'm not. There's too much for me to do today. I'm still a husband. I'm still a dad. I've got a job. One day, you might interview me and I'll be standing; wouldn't that be a story!

**Wright**

That'd be great. Thank you so much, Chad, for being a part of the program with us today. Thanks for offering us practical insight about hitching to the star of our own vision and using its power of vision to pull us forward.

Consider the horror of a life-threatening injury that ends up claiming your ability to walk. But, as we've seen today, that even confined to a wheelchair, Chad Hymas has, and is, accomplishing more than most people I know. How does he do it? According to him, the same way any of us can do it. It isn't complicated. Just decide that life is worth living and with that vision and focus—20/20 foresight—we have the ability to achieve any important goal and make a real difference regardless of obstacles that life throws our way.

Chad, thank you so much for being with us today on *Speaking of Success.*

**Hymas**

Thank you. It's been fun.

# About the Author

On April 3, 2001, Chad was involved in a serious accident leaving him a quadriplegic; however, Chad's dreams were not paralyzed that day. Since then Chad has done the following:

- Established Chad Hymas Communications, Inc., a professional speaking company designed to motivate businesses and corporations to look ahead with 20/20 foresight, allowing the power of their vision to pull them forward.
- The *Wall Street Journal* calls Chad Hymas one of the ten most inspirational people in the world!
- Last year Chad spoke at 160 different events, traveling just over 180,000 miles.
- Chad has shared his personal message and entertained many audiences from organizations such as Wells Fargo, Blue Cross Blue Shield, VastFX, IHC, Coca Cola, and the Utah Jazz.
- He is a member of the National Speakers Association and is a CSP (Certified Speaking Professional). A designation achieved by fewer than 8 percent in the speaking industry.
- Past president of the National Speakers Association, Utah chapter.
- Maintaining his hobby and dream of managing a 5,100 acre elk preserve with his father, Kelly.
- He has raced in marathons, and in the summer of 2003, Chad set a world record by wheeling his chair from Salt Lake City to Las Vegas (513 miles).
- Participating in wheelchair athletic competition including basketball, rugby, wheelchair racing, and officiating basketball (a dream come true).
- Spending many hours with other injured individuals in therapy, encouraging them to overcome their challenges, focus on dreams and make them a reality, and to love life for all that it has to offer.

Chad says his greatest accomplishment is that he remains a devoted husband to his loving wife, Shondell, and proud father to their three children Christian, Kyler, and new little Gracee!

### Chad Hymas
Chad Hymas Communications, Inc.
Phone: 435.843.5707 (office)
877.BOOK.CHAD (toll free)
Fax: 435.843.5010
E-mail: info@chadhymas.com
www.chadhymas.com
www.meetchadhymas.com (bureau friendly)

# Chapter 8

## PATRICIA CLASON

### David Wright (Wright)

Today we're talking with Patricia Clason. Patricia Clason is a professional speaker, trainer, coach, consultant, and writer. As owner and director of the Center for Creative Learning, the focus of her work is on alternative methods of teaching and learning that produce high quality results. Her search for the best in the technology of human resource development has taken her as a student on many adventures through traditional and not-so-traditional training programs.

An important aspect of Patricia's presentations is that she addresses the psychological perspectives and principles behind the practical tools that she teaches. Patricia shares personal and real stories so people know that her practical wisdom comes from experience, not just books and good ideas.

Patricia, you often quote the wise philosopher, Anonymous, as saying, "You won't know when you get there if you don't know where you are going." How did you know when you got there? How do you define success?

## Patricia Clason (Clason)

Success is the mastery of life—designing and creating a life with health, wealth, love, and creative self-expression in a flowing balance that works for me. As a result of my years of practice of Tai Chi Chuan, a Chinese martial art, I focus on principles and practicing those principles in order to master life.

In Tai Chi, we learn about the flow of the yin and yang—the empty and full—a flow that is constantly changing and adjusting. Mastering the flow means moving beyond resisting what life brings us and making it work *for* us.

When my daughter was young, my focus was more on raising her than building my business; that was a fulfilling and rewarding focus, a choice I will always be grateful I made. As she grew older and needed me to be there less, I shifted more of my focus to my business, building a client base and traveling more.

There are two key principles that permeate everything I teach: personal responsibility and full, free, and safe expression of emotion. These principles are also a consistent base under all of the teachings about success that I have read and experienced in my life.

One of the first things to be responsible for is the way we define success. Instead of taking on a definition of success from our parents, peers, or the media, each of us must choose how we will define success and experience satisfaction. There will always be someone who has more or less than you have, so comparing yourself to anyone else in order to gauge your success is a mistake. We all have talents that we express in a unique way. Not everyone can be a billionaire, powerful businessperson, politician, media star, or professional athlete. The roles needed to make our world work are many. If we each mastered doing what we do well with love, respect, excellence, and creativity, we would all have satisfaction and a lifestyle that fits us—in other words: Success.

Being in the moment—focusing *Now*—and doing our resourceful best is another important aspect of success. To call the result we achieve when making our best effort anything other than success requires moving out of the present moment into the past or future, comparing what is to what was or what could have been. Success isn't an end, a destination, or somewhere we are going. Success is being present to life in the moment and experiencing it to the fullest; we are always there and always arriving at the same time.

**Wright**

What does it mean to practice personal responsibility?

**Clason**

Success is directly related to one's willingness to be 100 percent personally responsible for one's life. When we blame anyone or anything else for *our* experience, *our* emotions, or *our* results, we give away *our* power to make changes and sculpt life to get the results we want.

At some level, we all know that we can't control other people or their actions. What we *can* do is take 100 percent of the responsibility for our choices, our actions and reactions, and our beliefs and emotions. These are some of the attitudes or behaviors of taking responsibility:

- Accepting what is—no blame, it just is,
- Instead of bragging or being prideful, simply owning our actions and results,
- Skipping the excuses, reasons, and justifications, and empowering ourselves by being accountable for our results— what we did or did not do,
- Repairing mistakes when necessary, and as soon as possible,
- Owning our beliefs, attitudes, and perceptions as just that—our beliefs, attitudes, and perceptions—not the absolute truth,
- Respecting others' beliefs, attitudes, and perceptions, and
- Changing our beliefs, thoughts, and actions in order to create different results.

Rather than waiting for someone else to do it for you, give it to you, or do it to you, or letting the world outside you determine your life, taking 100 percent responsibility gives you the opportunity to shape life into what you want it to be.

**Wright**

You talk about making core choices—fundamental choices—that affect the rest of our choices and actions. What are those core choices?

**Clason**

In order to have the life we went, there are certain choices we must make.

The first core choice is to *choose.*

We must choose what *we want* to make of our lives and then act on that choice. To not do so invites the world outside of us to determine our future, and just as surely to determine our dissatisfaction and struggle.

**The second core choice is to define our purpose or vision for life.**

Vision is our reason for being (*raison d'être* from the French). This vision or purpose is one without end—it lasts as long as we do. Once we have a vision, we then define our mission—how we will bring that vision into reality. Within that mission are the goals—the specific results we want to achieve along the way.

We also have to choose what kind of person each of us wants to be, and what qualities we want to develop in ourselves. These qualities are the values we hold that guide us spiritually in our choices and actions.

My personal values include:

- persistence and perseverance,
- patience,
- passion,
- flexibility,
- authenticity,
- compassion,
- curiosity,
- continuous learning,
- family/team consciousness,
- healthy boundaries,
- self-care,
- emotional intelligence,
- living life intentionally,
- respect,
- willingness to ask for and receive assistance,
- integrity and accountability,
- introspection (constantly examining strengths and weaknesses), and
- ethics.

My top three values are peace, love, and truth. I strive to make choices that are loving (even if it is sometimes tough love), truthful (in integrity), and that create peace.

The third core choice is to plan for success, using the tools proven to be effective over time in getting results.

Whether we are talking about building a business or a family, it is important to *have* a plan, *work* the plan, *review* the plan, *revise* the plan, and then begin the cycle again. As life brings us changes and challenges, the plan requires revision. That doesn't mean it was a bad plan or that we shouldn't have a plan. It is the nature of all plans that they change and grow over time.

As you work the cycle of planning, it is critical to continually re-orient yourself to your vision, mission, and values. Future pace: ask yourself, "What will my life be like five years, ten years, twenty years from now if I take this action, follow this path? Is that what I want? Can I live with myself and feel good about those results? Will my family and friends be proud of me?"

### The fourth core choice is to act.

Taking regular, consistent action on the plans that we create is necessary to get results. While we may occasionally be pleasantly surprised by a goal that just seems happen all by itself, we need to work our plan. Also, continual development of habits of thought and action that support our vision and mission make it easier to handle the down times (challenges) and help us create the up times (celebrations) that are a part of the roller coaster ride we call life.

### The fifth core choice is whether to play small or play large.

Playing small is about avoiding risk and holding back in fear. It's about withholding our talents and our potential to contribute. The result of playing small is that we live at the level of survival. We can be in "survival mode" even when we have a lot of money or other traditional measures of success yet we live in fear of loss, not truly enjoying or sharing life with others.

Playing large, on the other hand, is about taking a risk to make a difference—to contribute our talents and compassion to the world. It's about making a difference that helps create a better, safer world for others. In *Taking It Lightly,* the weekend emotional intelligence intensive I created, we say, "There is only one heart, and it matters to this one." This phrase is a combination of the concept of our being inter-dependent here on this planet (one heart) with the reality that making a difference for one affects all.

I love the story from Lauren Eiseley, *The Star Thrower,* which has been paraphrased into a very short story you have probably seen in many places. An observer sees a person on the beach early in the morning, throwing something into the sea. As the observer gets closer, it becomes apparent that the person is returning stranded starfish to the sea. The observer asks, "There are millions of starfish on this beach. You can help so few. Does it really make a difference? Does it matter?" The thrower responds, "Oh yes, it matters to this one."

There is a ripple effect each time a person reaches out in kindness or contributes to the world in a positive way, just like the ripples that flow when we throw a stone into the pond.

Playing large is not about how much money, acknowledgment, or media attention we receive. It is making your contribution regardless of the risk that it may not be popular or welcomed by some, or that it may not be seen or acknowledged by *anyone*. In fact, playing large is often focused on others—helping them to become co-creators in their lives. Instead of impressing others with your presence, it leaves them feeling good and strong and capable, impressed with themselves.

### Wright

What do you mean by the principle of full, free, and safe expression of emotion?

### Clason

Full, free, and safe emotional expression equals Emotional Intelligence. Neuroscience researchers and psychologists are now telling us that 80 percent of success in any job is determined by the level of emotional intelligence within the individual. I taught full, free, and safe emotional expression for twenty years before Daniel Goleman's book made "emotional intelligence" an everyday term.

The four key competencies of emotional intelligence as defined by Daniel Goleman include: knowing one's own emotions, being able to manage one's emotions, being able to relate to emotions in others, and being able to manage relationships.

Full expression of emotion does not mean explosive emotion. It means feeling emotions fully and expressing them safely. As we learn to experience our own emotions and the emotions of others safely, our relationships become easier and more satisfying. We develop ways to communicate even the deep emotions, which allows us to create intimacy, heal old wounds, or enrich our relationships. The flow of emotion—which is literally energy in motion—brings more aliveness.

Many people, and even some modern psychology texts, refer to anger, sadness, and fear as the "negative emotions," implying that they are bad and wrong. Yet every emotion has a time and a place; they are all natural responses to life's experiences. Even anger is useful and can be felt and expressed in healthy ways without becoming violence. When we are safe with all of our emotions and they can flow freely, they don't build to toxic levels, resulting in violence or depression. Instead, we experience the flow of life and joy and gratitude for all of our experiences.

My own process of developing my emotional intelligence escalated with a weekend intensive in 1983 called *Understanding Yourself and Others*. I became an instructor for that program, and then in 1986 wrote a new weekend program called *Taking It Lightly*. Since 1983, I have taught over 350 weekend intensives. Doing all of those weekends gave me an abundance of experience in feeling and expressing my own emotions, as well as developing and fine-tuning my emotional intelligence skills. Several thousand people have graduated from *Taking It Lightly*. It has been so gratifying to see their lives transform as they develop their emotional intelligence and live their lives with personal responsibility. This is, next to raising my daughter, my greatest success.

**Wright**

In your experience, what keeps people from success?

**Clason**

*Being unwilling to practice—to do the work.* One of the biggest obstacles to success is an unwillingness to do the work necessary to practice the principles. We often become sidetracked by techniques or offerings for quick success. We can be distracted or misled by the allure of immediate gratification; yet in the end this is not satisfying. It only causes us to want more and want it faster, like any other addiction.

We learn everything through repetition and practice, which develops the neural pathways that become our hard-wired patterns and beliefs about life. These neural pathways allow us to function easily because they allow us to do many things in life on autopilot. It took us time and practice to master walking, talking, eating, writing, reading, driving, and many other things we do in life. Can you imagine how difficult life would be if you had to *think about* tying your shoes, taking a step, or hitting return on a keyboard every time you did it?

Success is the same way. It takes time and practice, working the principles until you *become* the principles. My Tai Chi instructor always said, "Practice, practice, practice." Eventually the principles are integrated in you and you have mastery. Success then becomes as easy as taking a walk.

The other major obstacle for most people is the set of beliefs they hold about themselves, life, success, money, work, relationships, etc., that were formed as a result of their childhood experiences in these areas. These beliefs are usually fear-based and over time become automatic habits of thought and action—so automatic that many times people don't even recognize that these beliefs are running their lives. How often do you let a four-year-old make a decision that runs your life? Here's a secret: *people do it all the time!* Their lives are running on decisions that were made early in life and now are so subconscious that they are rarely, if ever, questioned. My Tai Chi instructor had another saying: "Pay attention, pay attention, pay attention!"

The most common self-defeating belief is, "I am not good enough," and it has many variations, usually with the same result—some form of self-sabotage. If we want success, we must become aware of our self-defeating decisions and replace them with ones that work *for* us!

### Wright

Once you have success you're done, right?

### Clason

No. Just like a martial art, if you don't continue to practice, you become rusty—not as flexible or strong.

Life will continue to offer challenges, obstacles, and changes for you to handle. In my experience, it's like a video game—we master one level, and then reach another where the obstacles are more challenging. So, in order to master the game, we continue to develop higher levels of skill and mastery. This comes from practice, practice, practice.

### Wright

Do we have a responsibility to others in our success?

### Clason

I believe we *do* have a responsibility to others—the responsibility of giving. There are actually three facets to this responsibility.

The first responsibility is to be a role model and mentor who teaches and empowers co-creators, who is accountable and holds others accountable, who lives in balance, and celebrates the successes of others. It is having gratitude for what we have been given and sharing the wealth (tangible or intangible) with others. I call this the responsibility to contribute or *to give back.*

One interesting aspect of success is that it attracts to itself scrutiny, jealousy, sabotage, and other negative energies of those unwilling to create their own success. We have a responsibility to continue acting in alignment with in our vision, mission, and values despite the often unconscious attempts of others to take us down because their misery loves company. This is the second responsibility of giving: *to not give up.*

In success, we can also be tempted with greed—the lust for the accomplishment and the resulting attention or benefits. Our responsibility is to pursue a practical and profitable plan for a worthy purpose, rather than doing "whatever" *just* to get the money or recognition. This is the third responsibility of giving: *to not give in.*

**Wright**

Who are the success role models who inspired you?

**Clason**

One of my role models is Earl Nightingale who said, *"Success is the progressive realization of worthy purpose."* Hearing this was a turning point for me as I began to recognize that success was not material things—the big house, fur coats, fancy cars, or lots of money. It rang true for me in my heart that a worthy purpose was the reason for living and true success was about living out that purpose, whether it included material wealth or not. There are many financially wealthy people who live simple lives and find their success and satisfaction in playing large and making the world a better place to live.

James Allen said, *"To put away aimlessness and weakness, and begin to think with purpose, is to enter the ranks of the strong ones who only recognize failure as one of the pathways to attainment; who make all conditions serve them, and who think strongly, attempt fearlessly, and accomplish masterfully."* This quote also had a deep impact on me. It reminds me that I will make mistakes, fall short, or fail, and that it is simply another step along the path. If I don't judge my failures as *bad*, or *myself* as bad for having them, then I can learn from my mistakes. If I am willing to learn, I won't fear failure. Learning also helps me be satisfied with my results and keeps me moving forward.

Fred Lehrman said, *"Why are you pretending you are not great?"* Fred was my original Tai Chi instructor; one of his gifts to me was this question. He taught me about owning my greatness—that I have a gift for the world, that my gift makes a difference, and that I can be proud of this gift.

We often compare ourselves with others who have done more, have more, do it better, etc. Or we think that we have to accomplish big things, be recognized by the world, or be famous. Making a difference one person at a time is as important to the planet as impacting thousands at a time. Our names don't have to be in the media or history books for us to have made a great contribution.

Mother Theresa said, *"Do it anyway."* Mother Theresa is cited as having a poem on her wall called *Anyway* that was about doing what was right regardless of the response of others. I learned from her that living my life following my vision matters to the one heart, one person at a time. She did what she believed was the right thing for her to do in alignment with her values and spirituality. She is also an example of success and satisfaction that is not materially based.

There are those who will succeed in the material world, some in great measure. There are those who will succeed in other aspects of life. Some will succeed at being good parents and raising good children, others succeed at finding a job that they love or a vocation that contributes to the world. Living a simple, satisfying life is also success. It is not ours to judge another person's path of success or to compare it to our own or to anyone else's path.

### Wright

Is there anything that you suggest people do and/or not do in their search for success?

### Clason

- Don't look for magic formulas as the easy way out. They don't work.
- Remember to nurture your relationships and your spirituality, or all that you achieve will still leave you feeling empty.
- Pay attention to your body—good health is critical to being able to enjoy the fruits of your success.

- Don't do anything just for the money. Selling your soul for material wealth will eventually destroy your creativity and passion, maybe even your physical health and relationships.
- Take action today—*now*. We do not know how many more seconds or days or years we have left to live. Make this moment and every moment the best it can be. Live it fully. Appreciate it fully.

*My parting wisdom is: The world is abundant with opportunity, like a deep, deep well of fresh water. You have a choice—will you just sip because you think there's not enough, or will you drink fully and freely with gratitude?*

# About the Author

For over thirty years, Patricia Clason has traveled across the continent doing speeches, workshops, and media appearances as a professional speaker, trainer, consultant, writer, and coach, giving over 4,000 presentations for corporations, associations, government agencies, and non-profit organizations. Now the owner and Director of the Center for Creative Learning, which offers programs for personal and professional development at offices in Milwaukee, Madison, and Detroit, Patricia has written many articles, training programs, and personal growth seminars. She hosted radio and television interview shows for ten years and is also a sought-after guest.

As a consultant and business coach she works with large and small companies as well as with individuals in the areas of start-up, marketing, management skills, and career building.

Patricia was the first to receive the Registered Corporate Coach designation from the National Association of Business Coaches (now the Worldwide Association of Business Coaches). *Ask the Coach,* Patricia's question and answer column on career coaching, appeared regularly in *Employment Times* and is currently on *MilwaukeeJobs.com.* Her articles are also often printed in business and trade publications and in online newsletters.

To keep all this together, and still have time for her family and herself, Patricia must truly practice what she teaches in the areas of communication, time and stress management, and motivation, as well as business marketing, management, emotional intelligence, and ethics.

**Patricia Clason**
Patricia Clason, LLC
Center for Creative Learning, LLC
2437 N Booth Street
Milwaukee, WI 53212
Phone: 414.374.5433
E-mail: patricia@lightly.com
www.patriciaclason.com
www.lightly.com

# Chapter 9

MARY WOLF

### David Wright (Wright)

Today we're talking with Mary Wolf. She is a speaker and strategic consultant specializing in working with people and their companies to achieve unparalleled success. She is a highly motivational force in helping people go beyond their personal expectations, and she is a strategic thinker who has the ability to keenly assess situations and deliver fast results.

Mary is founder of Mary Wolf Enterprises, LLC, and she brings twenty-five years of experience in organization and leadership development with Fortune 500 companies. She provides strategic consulting, executive coaching, talent alignment, leadership and management development, team enhancement, and training, as well as speaking engagements. Her programs are customized for high impact. She works in all industries and work environments. She is listed in *Who's Who of American Women,* and in the *Cambridge Who's Who Registry.* She has been on local radio, quoted in the *Wall Street Journal,* and has been the focus of newspaper business articles. She served as an executive women's delegate to China and a guest lecturer for Rider University. She serves on several organizations' boards of directors, and is active in many professional organizations.

Mary Wolf, welcome to *Speaking of Success.*

### Mary Wolf (Wolf)

Thank you David, thank you very much.

### Wright

So what has been your journey to success?

### Wolf

Well, David, I started out about twenty-five years ago. I had a small successful retail business and was also an adjunct professor at a community college when the Dean called me in one day and said he wanted to start a consulting piece to the college and he wanted me to head it up. This was a little foreign to me at the time for I had really no background in that field; but I'm not one to say no so I said I would be delighted to do it. I asked him to please send me to New York.

In New York I conducted some research, attended some seminars, and figured it all out. I then began my journey in consulting.

I found that I loved consulting because it combines the three areas I'm passionate about. One is business, two is people development, and three is learning. I found that this part of consulting and designing training programs and coaching people really turned me on so I applied for a job at RCA as a stand-up trainer; I was lucky enough to get that. I sold my retail business and started my journey to my career in organizational development.

I have found that my guiding path has always been the internal urges I feel—the areas of life that I feel very passionate about, the things I love to do, the kinds of things I'm willing to stay up all night for, to take risks. I'll put these into three major areas:

1. *Professional*—My barometers are these: am I doing the work I love? Am I making a difference? Am I respected and known for the work? Am I sought out by others?
2. *Personal*—Relationships with my family and friends are very, very important to me. I need those relationships to be wholesome, reciprocal, and very highly functioning. I work hard on that. I also value my good health, fitness, spirituality, and my emotional state. I want to be an emotionally healthy person.

3. *Financial*—I set my own targets and I create ways of getting there.

I set goals for myself every day and ask myself periodically, am I where I want to be? If not, what do I have to do to get there? And the peak of achieving success for me is to be the architect of my own life, to chart my own course, and to decide how I want to live my life, and then I make it happen.

**Wright**

Have you found that there is a secret ingredient successful people seem to have?

**Wolf**

Most definitely, and I've whittled them down to twelve key areas of success. One is that successful people have a bias toward action. They always ask themselves, how can I? They don't sit around and think about why this happened or why that happened. They're always questioning how they can do something and how they can conquer obstacles. They follow-up, they follow-through, they don't say what they're going to do without doing it. They take action and they're always anticipating everything that might be coming their way, they're always looking around the corner.

The second one is that successful people go inside to flourish outside. In other words, they set goals, they know their strengths, they know who and where their resources are, and they call on them. They adjust their sails in the direction of the strong winds that move them forward to achieving their goals. They're like mountain-climbers—they know they can rest and lean on their team when they're tired and not judge that as a weakness but as a strength in their climb to the top.

The third ingredient successful people have is they never stop learning and yearning for more. They know they will never reach the end—success is always a work in progress. Success is a journey and they enjoy the ride!

The fourth ingredient is woven through all successful people—their passion. They're always in touch with what they love to do, they surround themselves with people they love, and they create their plan around that.

Number five is successful people internally explore who they are as well as the world around them. They rely on their strengths and they have full confidence in themselves. They know where to turn when they need help; they know they cannot do everything themselves and they don't try. They capitalize on their talents and their strengths and they trust those around them to fill those gaps. The total picture is what counts with successful people.

Ingredient number six (another major ingredient) is that they have the courage to live out loud. It is a courageous act to put yourself out in the world and to stand up to criticism—there's going to be a lot of that—and there are a lot of unknowns. The secret here is that little ole belief in yourself and the knowledge that you are a winner no matter what—you can handle challenges that come your way. David, sometimes we just have to figure it out as it comes to us. Knowing how to do things and knowing how to take care of ourselves is also very important.

Number seven is that they put joy in their work. This comes from their passion and they work in that joy. Their work is not work, it's more like play. You'll find people who love what they do thrive on it, it shows, and it's contagious. People are attracted to them for this joy they provide and put out into the world.

Number eight is that successful people know what they stand for and what they don't stand for and they use their energy wisely.

Number nine is they always trust their gut. They check things out cognitively and intelligently but their decisions are usually swift. They use their intuition and they keenly apply their knowledge.

The tenth ingredient is that successful people are secure in their decisions even in the face of doubt. Again, they always trust their gut.

The eleventh ingredient is they use their energy to fight for what they believe in, not against what they don't believe in.

Number twelve—the final ingredient successful people have—is that they do not perceive a difference between what ifs and what is. Even though they certainly know that there is a "what if—" their passion and determination propel them forward. They love the uncharted course.

Those are my twelve keys to success, David.

**Wright**

So do you have a formula that has served you well?

**Wolf**

I do David. I surround myself with positive people from whom I can learn and people who can also learn from me. When I am with people who want to be around me it fortifies my strengths and it energizes me to challenge myself to rise to new heights.

Years ago I heard a statement that has resonated deeply with me to this day and it's this: "Successful people are willing to do what unsuccessful people are not." That's it in a nutshell. Successful people do what it takes to reach their goals and align values with their actions. They jump hurdles, they build bridges, they take risks, they hit brick walls, and they create innovative ways to get around them. They use detours as opportunities.

Successful people have clarity on what they say yes to and what they say no to and the consequences of both. Life comes at us quickly these days, everybody knows that, and successful people innately know what to grab onto and what to let go of; they do it quickly, never taking their eye off their goal.

So that sums up my little formula David.

### Wright

I know there are a lot of skills that go into being successful, but would you share with our readers at least three skills that you think are critical in creating a path to success?

### Wolf

Yes I will. One of the things that I've observed (and I certainly know within myself) is I just put one foot in front of the other and keep moving forward in the direction of my goals. I create clear actions every single day that move me forward. And here's another clue that I think is so critical in regard to successful people—they know when to rest and the benefits of play and I mean "play" in the true sense of the word. Play activates the right brain, which is your creative side. That can serve you well and help you be innovative and refreshed back on the job. These are some really critical skills that are not real tangible but that successful people really put into play.

The second one is that successful people have contingency plans and they're ready to activate them.

The third one is, as I said before, that they know who their resources are. They know who they can depend on and who has their best interests at heart. They know what skills and talents they need at any particular time and who has them; they then go after those who have those skills and talents.

**Wright**

So what has been your biggest challenge?

**Wolf**

Ah David, my biggest challenge is managing my emotions—my emotional intelligence. Change is inevitable but growth is optional and time and time again I have witnessed that managing emotions is the biggest downfall of people. Conversely, good management of emotions can contribute greatly to their success. Once again, it's a journey inward—checking into what's really going on inside, acknowledging it, accepting it, having insight about it, and making strong decisions not to display inappropriate behavior but rather to use your intellect to express your feelings in a thought-provoking way to move you forward.

Sometimes you just might be down for the count but know that you always have a choice. Although it might not be easy or obvious you will get another chance.

One of my mantras has been that old song, *The Gambler,* by Kenny Rogers. When you examine it, success is actually gambling or betting on yourself to win, so I like this song:

> "You got to know when to hold 'em,
> Know when to fold 'em,
> Know when to walk away and know when to run."

I say that in my head quite frequently and it serves me well. I remind myself daily that I only have so much energy to use that day and so I use it wisely. I make priority decisions around my daily goals that take me one step further to my big goals. I always know that there are going to be interruptions so I plan for them. That way I diminish my stress level, which as we all know consumes our energy. So I count on the unexpected every day because it's as sure as anything else to show up. I remind myself that when things seem insurmountable today they'll be a piece of cake tomorrow.

I also remind myself that the greatest success is paying it forward and doing that, there's always a bias toward action.

**Wright**

So how do you navigate the challenges that come your way and come out on top?

**Wolf**

Well, I really observe this keenly—some people let things happen but successful people *make* things happen. So I've learned how to ride the speed bumps in the road, when to slow down, and when and where to speed up. I reach out when I need to and I check out data, information, and knowledge. I then turn what I've learned into wisdom to shed light on the situation.

Sometimes you've just got to get away—sometimes that's the secret to success. Throw it in the proverbial pile, walk away, and do something totally and completely different. We get so entrenched in our own processes and thoughts. They can become a whirlpool that has its own power. We can lose perspective and getting away helps. Go to the movies when you're over the top. Go to the beach, take a hike, go for a bike ride, go shopping, go to a museum—do whatever it takes to give yourself the space you need when you need it. This is truly working with yourself and going inward so you can be effective outwardly.

**Wright**

How important do you think people skills are to success?

**Wolf**

Well, let me put it this way: is there anything—anything in the entire world—we do that doesn't ultimately involve people? I don't think so. Understanding differences and what your hot buttons are, what pushes your patience, how to interact with all types of people, and how to handle different behaviors so that you can create win-win situations are keys to all successes. Whatever we do we're working through people.

I live by the platinum rule. Most people know the golden rule, which is of course to "do unto others as you would have them do unto you." My platinum rule is "do unto others as they would have you do unto them," so I watch, I listen, I learn. Successful people are keen listeners.

**Wright**

So do you have any advice that you give to beginners?

**Wolf**

Yes I do, because it wasn't so long ago I felt like a beginner. My advice is to create your own definition of success. That's so important.

Everybody needs to have a personal definition of what success is for them.

Then make a list of the top 100 things you want to achieve in life, put them in priority order, create a timeline, identify steps that need to take place, identify possible obstacles and back-up plans, create your action plan with goals, dates, and just chip away at it every single day.

Another piece of advice I have is listen to those urges inside of you. Know what your passion is and know that passion is the fuel and your belief in yourself is the lubricant for your energy force.

Create your personal mission, vision, and value statement and keep it in front of you at all times no matter where you are. Put a copy on your desk, put a copy in your laptop, put a copy anywhere you go and keep it in front of you as a reminder.

Know what you stand for and what you stand against—that's so important.

Know that the biggest risk in life is really truly not taking a risk. Everyone is afraid but the successful do it anyway.

I love Stephen Covey's circle of control and circle of influence. We have to put our energy to work wisely and focus on our circle of control and know that a satisfying life of peace, joy, contentment, and happiness come ultimately from pushing ourselves to the limit. Create a life you love and when it's all said and done, look back and admire your canvas. You started with a blank one and created a masterpiece. It's uniquely yours.

Develop a quiet knowing that even in the face of adversity you can take control—the circle of control. Insulate yourself from negative forces, know that there is a safe haven and balance is the key so when you're tired, rest, play, and come back with gusto. Know that there's a high cost to doing nothing, much greater actually than taking risks. And live on purpose, know what your excellence is, observe, ask, and do, get feedback along the way.

Being productive is possible every minute. That may even mean reflection time, play time, down time; but you need to engage your creativity.

I like to form a coalition. I have an advisory board I use—people I turn to who will give me advice on the tough stuff.

Believe in yourself, in your natural intuitive capability and take quantum leaps.

Know what motivates you. Have a knowledge of what's important to you and develop the willingness to make the right trade-off. Discipline yourself to do what you don't really want to do at times.

Know that success is very personal as well as public. There will always be naysayers who usually sound like they really know that bad things are on the way and you know what, they just might be right; but put your energy into positive outcomes and go forward. Surround yourself with winners and people you can learn from. Challenge yourself, learn from the masters, internalize your success, build on it. In the end know you can do well by doing good.

**Wright**

So what would you consider your biggest motivator to be?

**Wolf**

I'd have to say it's my drive, my unwillingness not to give up, my ability to see the future, my ability to taste success before it materializes, and recreating over and over again something out of nothing.

**Wright**

So how do you know what you don't know?

**Wolf**

Ah, that's a good question. By paying keen attention to what's going on around me, by picking people's brains, by being curious, by admitting that I have a lot to learn. I have an 80/20 equation that looks something like this: I know 80 percent of what I need to know to be successful at what it is I want to achieve. The other 20 percent I either have resources for or I just simply don't know it, so I listen and I learn.

I have a little acronym that I'd like to share with you.

SUCCESS:
S—Start at the beginning.
U—Upward is always the path.
C—Clarity
C—Creativity
E—Enjoy the ride.
S—Strategize.
S—Stop to reflect.

**Wright**

What's next for Mary Wolf?

**Wolf**

Ah, what's next for Mary Wolf? I just want to keep on growing my company, Mary Wolf Enterprises. I'm very excited about this book. I intend to market it and do some public speaking.

I've also moved toward a new area of my life—real estate investment—so I intend to get really sharp on that end and make that another business of mine.

I'm also opening a new business called Street Smart Sales Academy®. This is specifically geared toward salespeople who work strictly on commission, which is a tough row to hoe.

I'm excited about that journey as well. Thanks for asking me David.

**Wright**

Well, what a great conversation. I really appreciate your taking all this time with me today to answer these questions.

**Wolf**

It was my pleasure.

**Wright**

Today we've been talking with Mary Wolf. She is a speaker and strategic consultant. She specializes in helping people and their companies achieve unparalleled successes. She is a highly motivational force in helping people go beyond their personal expectations. Mary is a strategic thinker who has the ability to keenly assess situations and deliver fast results. And I don't know about you, but I think she knows what she's talking about.

**Wolf**

Thank you David.

**Wright**

Thank you so much for being with us today, Mary, on *Speaking of Success.*

**Wolf**

It was my pleasure.

## About the Author

MARY WOLF, founder of Mary Wolf Enterprises, LLC, brings twenty-five years of experience in organization and leadership development with Fortune 500 companies. She provides strategic consulting, executive coaching, talent alignment, leadership and management development, team enhancement, and training, as well as speaking engagements. Her programs are customized for high impact. Mary works in all industries and work environments. She is listed in *Who's Who of American Women*, and in the *Cambridge Who's Who Registry*. She has been on local radio, quoted in the *Wall Street Journal,* and been the focus of newspaper business articles. She served as an executive women's delegate to China and a guest lecturer for Rider University. She serves on Boards of Directors, and is active in many professional organizations.

**Mary Wolf**
Mary Wolf Enterprises, LLC
7415 Fairlinks Court
Sarasota, FL  34243
Phone: 941.780.2578
Fax: 941.360.3196
E-mail: marywolf77@aol.com
www.mwolfenterprises.com

# Chapter 10

## DETRI MCGHEE

THE INTERVIEW

### David Wright (Wright)

Today we're talking with Detri L. McGhee. She is president of DLM and Associates. She has spent over twenty-five years in the financial services world as an insurance agent, a securities registered representative, a market development vice president, and then as training coordinator for one of the largest independent insurance firms in America. Detri led the on-site training of Wells Fargo Bank's first Insurance Representatives. Upon leaving that field, Detri owned a quilting shop for three years. Her Criticism Management System and its principles were compiled from over thirty years' experience in business and personal life. She now dedicates full time to sharing that information. Detri's CD and workbook are titled, *Criticism Management: Using the Cunning C-A-T to Tame the Dragon of Criticism.*

Detri, welcome to *Speaking of Success.*

### Detri L. McGhee (McGhee)

Thank you David, it's great to be here with you.

**Wright**

How do your Criticism Management principles and techniques propel people more quickly and easily toward success?

**McGhee**

Successfully handling criticism is a universal problem. From birth to death we are in danger of—and receive—criticism.

Just when we get wrapped in warm blankets and cuddled in Mom's arms for a moment, criticism hits. We are shuffled off in the arms of strangers only to be unwrapped and tugged upon. We experience one problem after another. At one point they stick us with a needle. Do we object? Most assuredly we do! So we are criticizing them for hurting us. And, we feel justified. After all, they criticized us first. They told us that our body wasn't perfect as it was and they needed to change it in some way. Well, of all the nerve. That *hurt!*

A simple test of whether any criticism management techniques and principles can benefit us is to ask this: "Do I ever get frustrated, depressed, mad, hurt, sad, defiant, incapacitated, or feel rejected? Or have I ever lost my temper?" You can bet that criticism or one of its siblings—grumbling, complaining, griping, or ingratitude—is at the root of the problem. Upon close inspection we can see that criticism in one form or another is included in any negative, painful situation of life. From birth to death it continues. At every turn we're faced with people telling us what to do and how to do it, where to go, how to get there, and even *when* to be there. We are told who we are and who we should become, what to learn, and how to learn it.

As we travel through our world, seldom do we feel that we are doing things right. In today's world many people don't even *know* how to define "right." Even the most self-confident, powerful, charismatic people in the world know how criticism stings.

The natural, undeveloped temperament of my youth included a much-too-deep desire to please everyone. I had a feeling that no matter what went wrong with anyone in my life—a loved one, classmate, coworker, or friend—it was somehow my fault. I felt that I should have been able to avoid the problem or at least fix it quickly and to everyone's complete satisfaction. That's a no-win situation. It took me quite a few years of heartache to realize that fact. Even today I sometimes feel twinges of inferiority or guilt when the people around me aren't happy.

Accompanying those feelings was the problem that criticism tended to incapacitate me—to make me want to hibernate and to run from trying. It was years before I found out that I was not alone. There was also this nagging *fear of success* that was as strong in me as any fear of failure. Actually, it was even stronger. I really didn't have much fear of failure. I had been told that I should just get up and try again, learn what I could and apologize sincerely if appropriate. Like the old song lyrics, "Pick yourself up, dust yourself off, and start all over again." My parents and teachers *expected* me to succeed and allowed me a reasonable number of mistakes along the way.

But when it came to adult life, I observed a different set of rules. I saw that failure was common, even pitied. People often reach out to you. Mediocrity is acceptable; it goes unnoticed so to speak. But with real success there is a heavy backlash to endure. Often, the one at the top is a target for everyone else. Just look at sports. People root for the underdog and then if they become too successful you will hear many people say, "I hope they get creamed. I'm sick of them winning." Then there's the sad truth that sometimes success does change people so they really *do* deserve some criticism. Deserved or not, people who excel will receive criticism—and lots of it.

For those dealing with failure right now, criticism management techniques can help to pinpoint the cause and uncover a strategy for turning that failure into success. For those in the midst of success, sometimes this wisdom is needed even more. In the search for and discovery of these criticism management principles I also learned that as we mature we *should be* evolving into a balanced personality that develops our natural strengths and works through our natural weaknesses. I deeply wanted that balance in my life and through seeking that, the concept of Criticism Management was born.

### Wright

"Criticism Management"—I don't believe I've heard that exact term before. Did you coin that phrase?

### McGhee

Well David, I guess perhaps I did. I don't remember hearing the term before I began using it. Because of my career, I've studied a lot about communication and sales skills. I grew up professionally on Earl Nightingale's tapes and self-help books. I've seen some work on how to give criticism but I have never seen any in-depth discussion on how to take criticism—*any* and *all criticism,* constructive or not—and make it work *for* me instead of trying to ignore it or letting it harm me.

In trying to learn from all the success gurus, another problem invariably cropped up for me. Without fail they all gave strong advice to always, always, *always* avoid negative people. Even my favorite early mentor, Dr. Norman Vincent Peale, consistently advised avoiding negative people. He said negative people bring us down, try to crush our dreams, and offer only discouragement.

Of course, he was right. However, what if that negative person is someone you love, right in your own family, with whom you don't *want* to sever your relationship? Are we doomed then to depression and failure because we spend so many hours with someone like that? Isn't there some wisdom in all of creation that can help us to succeed and have happy, fulfilling lives while dealing with (rather than deleting) that relationship? That is an important function of criticism management techniques. *That* is what makes it worth the work to discover the system, the techniques, and the principles.

### Wright

Was there a crisis time that actually started you writing these concepts down?

### McGhee

Yes, David, there was. In my early thirties I received some substantial and undeserved criticism (at least, that's the way I viewed it). I reacted to it rather inappropriately. Because of my reaction not only did I have to deal with undeserved, incorrect criticism, but I had to acknowledge some deserved, correct criticism of my inappropriate reaction!

I'm not sure what hurts more, David—undeserved criticism that's *wrong* or deserved criticism that is *right!* That's a little like asking what hurts more—a broken leg or a broken arm. The answer, of course, is, "Whichever you have at the moment."

Through the years, I have found that the best way for me to really learn from something—to learn how I truly feel—is to put my concerns and questions on paper, then write and rewrite and *re*-rewrite my answers to those issues *until even I agreed with the answer.*

Who said it first? I don't know, but the first person I remember hearing say this was Mark Victor Hansen. He said, *"Don't just think it—ink it!"*

**Wright**

So this material was originally developed for your *personal* use. How did you find out that others would be so interested in learning to handle criticism more productively?

**McGhee**

Through the years, I've shared bits and pieces in various places—with a women's network group that I co-founded, the local Life Underwriters Association, church groups, a women's conference, and bank management teams. People always responded positively and added to my understanding that I had only *begun* to see the tip of the iceberg where this topic is concerned.

For instance, one year, as secretary of the local Life Underwriters Association, I worked with the group officers as we diligently sought to increase membership. Our programs were very important in that process. At one of those meetings a mild panic set in when it became clear to our vice president that the program presenter was a no-show. He was familiar with some of my Criticism Management principles and he turned to me just *beaming* with this great idea he had suddenly had. He said, "Detri, get up and share what you told me about Criticism Management. It's good stuff. Save my backside here, okay?" So I took my outline, which I had printed on the back of my business card, and winged it. About twenty minutes later we adjourned.

Immediately, one of the most successful and respected agents who was approaching retirement and who was also the kindest, most supportive mentor to all of us, approached me. I was taken aback, David. He literally had tears in his eyes. He said, "Detri, how I wish I had heard that fifty years ago! I see so many missed opportunities, especially with my family. Thank you for sharing that." As he continued to speak I began to realize that he had heard some things *that I hadn't said!* He had applied these principles to *his* life and while I was envisioning and speaking of a C-A-T that looked like a lion to me, he was seeing a Bengal tiger!

His reaction touched me and made me dig deeper. Once that happened I began to discover how many famous and powerful people struggle in this area, sometimes in professional relationships and sometimes in personal relationships.

**Wright**

"Famous people"? Will you give us a few examples?

**McGhee**

One of the first that comes to my mind is Jessica Savitch. Do you remember her?

**Wright**

As a matter of fact, yes, I do!

**McGhee**

She was so popular and beautiful. She was a newswoman on the rise in the world of journalism at a time when Barbara Walters was about the only truly successful woman in the broadcast industry. Jessica met an untimely death in a car accident. As I read a book about her life (I believe it was *Golden Girl* by Alanna Nash), Jessica seemed so perfect on television with the cameras rolling. Yet, when the camera went off she could fly into hateful tirades and venomous outbursts. She was apparently unstable and rather unsuccessful in personal relationships. One insight that jumped off the pages of the book at me was when she said that she could not get inner peace because she never came to terms with the criticism she received as a child from her father.

I thought, "Oh, if we could all *truly feel* what our words infuse into another soul, perhaps we would praise more, love more, listen more, speak less, and do what my mom always advised, *'If you can't say something nice, just keep your mouth shut!'* "

Mark Victor Hansen is another example. I heard him speak many years ago in Pine Bluff, Arkansas. He was great—energetic, upbeat, encouraging—yet he later said that during those early years he had a lot of problems promoting his own books and other materials. He said that *he feared being criticized*—that people might say he was just out for the money and pushing his own agenda. Can you imagine that—someone with his gifts and talents with that fear? It just blew my mind! I began to realize that I was not alone, I really wasn't.

And, another is Oprah. Do you remember when she experienced the controversy and the lawsuit about her comments concerning eating beef?

**Wright**

Yes, I do.

**McGhee**

Well, all that led to her professional friendship with Dr. Phil and we know what happened there. But wouldn't you think that someone as brilliant and "together" as Oprah would already have all the answers? Naïvely, I did.

**Wright**

I read in your materials that you have some strong opinions regarding annual job performance reviews. Well, just let me quote you if I may: "Inadequate Criticism Management skills virtually *guarantee* that annual job performance reviews, at their *best*, are useless exercises consuming valuable time, energy, and emotions, and, at their worst, they are monsters of destruction." Will you tell us how you came to feel so strongly about this?

**McGhee**

Well, you know what they say, "Been there, done that." I probably wrote that right after an annual job performance review. (Laughter.)

Actually, I have never had a bad job performance review. But, I do remember one year, even after I heard several nice things, some compliments and things looked fine, there was *one suggestion for improvement*. And, in my mind, that *one suggestion* canceled out all the praise I'd just heard. Of course it shouldn't have . . . but that wasn't the issue! The fact was: *it did!* If I had known *then* what I know *now,* I could have enjoyed the praise and then I could have *wisely used the suggestion* to propel me further, faster. If I had chosen wisely, I could have made that suggestion (criticism!) into a speedy growth process.

Anyone who has worked in an office environment can testify as to how tense and worried employees are when yearly review time grows near. Everyone is edgy. Some people come back from their sessions in tears or red-faced with anger. Others never hear a word their supervisor says unless they talked about a raise. Some overreact at the least suggestion for improvement (as I unwisely did) and others overlook valid criticism, determined to believe that if the boss says anything negative that he or she "has it in for them."

I don't know who had this idea first, but I really like it. Let's have "Reverse Job Performance Reviews"—the employee gets to tell the boss what the boss can do to make things better. It probably wouldn't work too well in most cases unless the boss applied Criticism Management techniques first in his or her daily life.

Are you familiar with Bill Schorr's comic strip *The Grizzwells*—poppa bear Gunther and his little porcupine friend Pierpoint?

**Wright**

Yes. I like that one.

**McGhee**

My very favorite is when Gunther's little friend, Pierpoint, asked, "How do *you* handle criticism, Gunther?" Big old papa bear Gunther said, "Hmm. Gosh little buddy, I don't *know*. No one has ever had *the nerve* to criticize me before. Why? You got a problem with that!?" And little Pierpoint quickly and wisely replied, "Nope. Uh-uh. Nada. Zip. No way."

Sadly, though, most managers and bosses come across to their employees just like big papa bear Gunther—"Do not *dare* criticize *me!*" As I watched the fear and dread in my own life and in the lives of friends and coworkers, I thought about how much wasted time, energy, and emotions were generated. I was strongly encouraged to keep digging and to find some ways to first of all help myself and then to help others cope with life's difficult situations. No, not just "cope"— I wanted to *find success* in the midst of life's difficulties. The Criticism Management principles have been of great help to me. I know they can be for others, too.

**Wright**

Tell our readers a little about this "C-A-T with the power to tame the dragon of criticism." What's that all about?

**McGhee**

David, I am a very simple person. I wanted a tool that I could use that would be easy to remember. You know, advancing age does that to us—we're lucky if we can remember our age! Anyway, I wanted a tool that was easy to remember, simple to apply, and yet powerful enough to effect change right away. I also wanted it to be so durable, flexible, and useable that it would grow with me, year by year.

The C-A-T stands for three steps in the evaluation technique that can be applied to any criticism to make it work for us. The "C" stands for Categorize, the "A" stands for Analyze, and the "T" stands for Take action. So many applicable analogies came to me when I thought of a cat. When you think of a cat, David, what does your mind's eye see?

**Wright**

Well, I have three cats.

**McGhee**

So you see a housecat?

**Wright**

Yes. This is not a philosophy that I thought up—it was on a t-shirt I saw one time that said, "Dogs have owners and cats have staff."

**McGhee**

That is so true! Some people do see a housecat or a little kitten. Someone might see Garfield or the big black cat of Halloween. Sometimes when I think of a cat (of course, now I'm always linking it mentally with criticism) I see a massive Bengal tiger or a feisty bobcat or even a fierce lion—the king of the jungle.

I got to thinking, as I thought about the cats, how would I like to be like a cat? It is said they have nine lives and that sounded pretty good on some days. Also, no matter how they fall, they always seem to land on their feet.

Then I observed that we are already like them in a lot of ways. Like people, cats come in infinite varieties—each kitten different from any other—and they're so sweet when they're cuddling. But even the youngest kitten can bite to the bone if they're threatened. Unfortunately, I know this from personal experience. I once tried to wash pesticide off a kitten that was just days old. It had been accidentally sprayed and I promise you, it is not a good idea to put a kitten in water, no matter how limp and lifeless it may appear.

Also, like our tongue, you can't totally tame a cat. Like our mind, a cat can't be completely kept from wandering. I also got to thinking, have you ever seen anyone herd cats? It is just not going to happen. Then I thought of the big cats—the lion (king of his domain) and the tiger who struts in fear of nothing. The analogies keep coming even now.

So, just how do we start to conquer a criticism? The first thing to do is to write down the criticism as we see it. And then, as the C-A-T is used for evaluation, we follow a simple outline where each of the three sections is further broken down into a set of two to four subquestions that trigger our thought process.

Basically, here's the entire formula:

1. **Categorize**—Break the criticism into bite-sized pieces. Take each part and ask, is it:
   a. Correct or Incorrect
   b. Deserved or Undeserved
   c. Solicited or Unsolicited
   d. From a Friend or Foe
2. **Analyze**—In this step we learn how to get to the root of the problem.
   a. Take your categories in step one and analyze each part. (The CD and workbook amplify the process and explain the importance of each category.)
   b. Re-assess the steps and *be honest until it hurts*. (It can help to pretend it is a criticism you *gave* rather than *received.*)
3. **Take Action**—Whether we want to or not, we are going to do something with every criticism we receive.
   a. Ignore It. We may *try* to ignore it, but that's like ignoring a donkey that comes into your living room, sits down in your lap, and won't get up—it is virtually impossible.
   b. Get Angry, Get Even, or Get Ulcers. Or, maybe give ulcers to someone else. This is the most common and most unwise option. It is usually followed with attempting Step 3.a.: Ignore It.
   c. Take Positive Action (this is our goal):
      i. Discard it with a clear mind or,
      ii. Use it for profit.

When you see the system in its entirety you begin to see why each step is important and then you personalize it to fit your temperament and current life needs.

At first glance, we might think step one, Categorizing, and step two, Analyzing, are basically the same thing. But in the categorizing element of handling criticism we'll learn to be very detached. We are merely breaking the criticism into bite-sized pieces necessary to "eat this elephant." Then in step two we will dissect each category personally, deeply, and honestly. Here is where we learn how to get to the root of the problem, to dispose of any chaff properly and completely, then salvage each grain of truth or wisdom for our own gain.

Let's quickly examine the deserved or undeserved section. Parts of the criticism might fit into each category. We need to consider that.

Just because the criticism was undeserved doesn't mean we're wise to ignore it. Within that situation might be the seeds of greatness. Wisdom may be there that is unavailable to us from anywhere else. Where each part fits will have a great impact on the final outcome of what we will *do* with that part of criticism. And remember—we *will do something* with every criticism we receive. The key is to do the right thing with each part so that we are benefited and not harmed.

My goal in seeking wise Criticism Management is two-fold: (1) Gain from everything of value that comes into my life, even if it comes from criticism and, (2) Recognize when something is useless and throw it away.

Here is a little trick I have to play on myself from time to time when I have a nagging thought or hurt feeling that I just can not seem to dispose of or release: I pretend it is an empty toothpaste tube, therefore, I can and should throw it away without guilt or remorse.

David, my mom and I are both really bad pack rats. Sometimes we've even been known to save empty paper towel and bathroom tissue tubes. (Did you know they make great stands for paper dolls and fabulous spy glasses?) But, even Mother and I don't save empty toothpaste tubes. They're totally useless. Trash! I don't remember how many I've tossed away because I don't care. I send them to destruction without a pause.

Sometimes turning loose of painful situations or comments or criticisms and so forth is not easy. Sometimes I have to help myself. After I have taken a criticism through the C-A-T process, and if I find it totally useless but nevertheless painful, I have been known to take the written criticism and envision it to be an empty toothpaste tube. I'll take it in my hand, I'll smile at it, I may even speak to it, saying something like, *"I have* total control *over you. You are worse than worthless to me. You are in my way staying here. You are g-o-n-e, gone for good—for my good!"* And then I toss it in the trash. If it has been a particularly painful criticism I might have a really long, nasty speech for it. I have been known to take the trash outside to the bin right that moment.

So, I work through each step, and once it is complete, I have a guaranteed positive result if I follow the principles, even if that result is being able to finally turn loose of the pain that the criticism caused.

**Wright**

I am wondering, Detri, this sounds like it *could* be a very time-consuming and lengthy learning process. How long does it take a person to *profitably use* this information?

**McGhee**

That's a very good question, David. The neat thing about this information is that we learn something from day number one. If we just pay attention to the concepts and principles presented we will keep learning and benefiting from that knowledge until the end of our days.

If I may, let me illustrate how it works with an analogy. Do you remember when you learned to drive a car?

**Wright**

Yes, I certainly do.

**McGhee**

I just soaked it up because I wanted to get all the benefits of that ability. I was young and I wanted to go! Of course it took time and effort. I made some silly mistakes along the way but it was exciting from the very first day. I hate to think how my life would have been all these years living in rural America if I had been unable to drive.

It is similar to learning to play golf, or swimming, or parenting, or the sales process. We learn as we go. What may start out tedious and even feel strange at first can be, as in the case of golf, a life-enhancing project, even *fun*.

When I get in the car now I don't even think about how to start it or which pedal is the brake. The myriad of little things I learned earlier automatically go to work for me and I simply begin to drive. Even relatively new golfers don't have to think, "Now, how do I put the ball on the tee?" The principle, once learned, becomes a habit.

In a similar manner, once you have become familiar with the Criticism Management Techniques and experienced the exciting, positive results of this knowledge, it becomes ingrained into your thinking process. From then on, when criticisms, suggestions, ideas, or complaints come your way, you will find yourself automatically responding to them in a more positive, helpful way.

Remember my goal? It was to create a tool that was easy to remember, simple to apply, and powerful enough to effect change right away, yet so durable, flexible, and useable that it would grow with me year by year.

**Wright**

I understand that your original subtitle was changed from "Using the Cunning C-A-T" to "*Slay* the Dragon of Criticism" to "Using the Cunning C-A-T to *Tame* the Dragon of Criticism." What made you decide that it was better to "tame" these dragons than to "slay" them?

**McGhee**

That was one of those "ah-ha!" moments. I was years into this process when it dawned on me that I still wanted to "kill" all the criticism and negativity and complaining that came into my life. In my mind it was a nasty, mean old dragon and it deserved to die! Then one day I thought: "If I found a dragon—*a real, live dragon*—would it be worth more to me if I killed it or if I tamed it?" I thought, "How *blind* I have been!" Criticism isn't bad; it is my reaction to it that determines its value and effect on me. It's a fact of life. I'm making a bumper sticker that says, "Criticism happens."

Criticism is often disguised as a comment.

I remember when I was new in sales—insurance sales, at that. I heard every insurance joke imaginable, over and *over!* People would tell me, "I could *never* be a salesperson." I felt I needed to defend my career choice at first. Now? I would probably smile and sweetly say, "Well, you know, you're probably right. It *does* take a *really special person* to do this job."

Criticism may come as a suggestion: "Perhaps you should not wear pink."

Sometimes it is disguised as a rule: "To work here, you will have to cut that hair, young man."

Or, it might come as a question, "Are you really going to wear *that?*"

Well, anyhow, David, I want this journey-making to continue and grow. I also hope and pray that other people will be blessed by this insight and share their wisdom with me, too. So, I decided to give away my C-A-T outline. I placed it on my Web site along with some of my favorite training pieces, all as a gift from me to anyone who would take the time to consider the Criticism Management system.

**Wright**

You're *giving away* your C-A-T outline?

**McGhee**

Yes. I want this information available to anyone who wants to help themselves or others. I know that having just the outline and illustrations given on the Web site will help some people. I also know that there is a plethora of valuable information that is provided in the training programs, on the CD, and in the workbook that isn't available anywhere else.

**Wright**

The more we talk, the more ways I see how just about everyone can benefit from understanding these Criticism Management techniques.

**McGhee**

I couldn't agree with you more.

**Wright**

Who do *you* think will benefit most from your work?

**McGhee**

Oh, probably human beings from age five to ninety-five! Seriously, the speeches, training workshops, CD, and workbook are geared toward adults and older teens. Whether applied to work or personal life, the principles are the same. Each on-site workshop is tailor-made for the profession, industry, or group involved. Because of my career background I have somewhat of an insider's understanding of the insurance, securities, banking, and medical professions, from the CEO and Board to the janitors. As a marketing VP, I had to make presentations to the CEOs and Boards. I also trained the salespeople on sales skills and products. In addition, every employee and Board member had to be trained on referral techniques and compliance issues. It was extremely challenging and interesting to develop training concepts that would reach people at *their learning level.*

I have a true appreciation for and understanding of salespersons, managers, Board members, quilt-lovers, owners of small businesses, parents, Christians, and women. And, oh yes, waitresses! That was my first job at age fourteen in our town's only hamburger joint.

**Wright**

What would you like to see in the future for this information?

**McGhee**

We do have a special edition coming out soon for women and one for Christians. My deep desire, David, is to see this information translated into a useable format for school children of all ages. The peer pressure and bullying that they are experiencing right now, as well as the lack of being able to properly respond to the various teaching methods, are greatly related to a lack of Criticism Management skills. We just have to get this information on their level and make it fun.

Come to think of it, the C-A-T is a really good beginning. What child isn't fascinated by kittens, and lions, and tigers! *Oh my!*

**Wright**

What an interesting conversation. I've learned quite a bit here today and I can't wait for this book to get in the hands of our readers. I think you can help them immensely.

**McGhee**

Thank you. It's been a lot of fun working on this project and visiting with you.

**Wright**

I really appreciate all this time you've spent with me. It was nice of you to take the time to answer all these questions.

Today we've been talking with Detri McGhee. She has spent over twenty-five years in the financial services world as an insurance agent, securities registered rep, and in the corporate market. She is now dedicating full time to sharing the information she has accumulated over her past thirty years of experience. Her CD and workbook that she has alluded to are titled, *Criticism Management: Using the Cunning C-A-T to Tame the Dragon of Criticism,* which is very interesting—at least I think it is. I look forward to learning even more!

# About the Author

DETRI L. MCGHEE, CLU, CHFC, conducts workshops and training sessions and enjoys speaking to a wide variety of groups using tailor-made applications in Criticism Management. Her CD book and workbook are titled, *CRITICISM MANAGEMENT: Using the Cunning C-A-T to Tame the Dragon,* and are available by phone, mail, or through her Web site. Special discounts apply if you mention this book.

**Detri L. McGhee, CLU, ChFC**
President
DLM & Associates
20161 US Hwy. 425 South
Star City, AR 71667
Phone: 870.370.0160 / 870.628.1464
E-mail: detri@criticismmanagement.com
www.criticismmanagement.com

# Chapter 11

JACK CANFIELD

THE INTERVIEW

**David E. Wright (Wright)**
Today we are talking with Jack Canfield. You probably know him as the founder and co-creator of the *New York Times* number one best-selling *Chicken Soup for the Soul* book series. As of 2006 there are sixty-five titles and eighty million copies in print in over thirty-seven languages.

Jack's background includes a BA from Harvard, a master's from the University of Massachusetts, and an Honorary Doctorate from the University of Santa Monica. He has been a high school and university teacher, a workshop facilitator, a psychotherapist, and a leading authority in the area of self-esteem and personal development.

Jack Canfield, welcome to *Speaking of Success.*

**Jack Canfield (Canfield)**
Thank you, David. It's great to be with you.

**Wright**

I talked with Mark Victor Hansen a few days ago. He gave you full credit for coming up with the idea of the *Chicken Soup* series. Obviously it's made you an internationally known personality. Other than recognition, has the series changed you personally and if so, how?

**Canfield**

I would say that it has and I think in a couple of ways. Number one, I read stories all day long of people who've overcome what would feel like insurmountable obstacles. For example, we just did a book *Chicken Soup for the Unsinkable Soul.* There's a story in there about a single mother with three daughters. She contracted a disease and she had to have both of her hands and both of her feet amputated. She got prosthetic devices and was able to learn how to use them. She could cook, drive the car, brush her daughters' hair, get a job, etc. I read that and I thought, "God, what would I ever have to complain and whine and moan about?"

At one level it's just given me a great sense of gratitude and appreciation for everything I have and it has made me less irritable about the little things.

I think the other thing that's happened for me personally is my sphere of influence has changed. By that I mean I was asked, for example, a couple of years ago to be the keynote speaker to the Women's Congressional Caucus. The Caucus is a group that includes all women in America who are members of Congress and who are state senators, governors, and lieutenant governors. I asked what they wanted me to talk about—what topic.

"Whatever you think we need to know to be better legislators," was the reply.

I thought, "Wow, they want me to tell them about what laws they should be making and what would make a better culture." Well, that wouldn't have happened if our books hadn't come out and I hadn't become famous. I think I get to play with people at a higher level and have more influence in the world. That's important to me because my life purpose is inspiring and empowering people to live their highest vision so the world works for everybody. I get to do that on a much bigger level than when I was just a high school teacher back in Chicago.

**Wright**

I think one of the powerful components of that book series is that you can read a positive story in just a few minutes and come back and revisit it. I know my daughter has three of the books and she just reads them interchangeably. Sometimes I go in her bedroom and she'll be crying and reading one of them. Other times she'll be laughing, so they really are "chicken soup for the soul," aren't they?

**Canfield**

They really are. In fact we have four books in the *Teenage Soul* series now and a new one coming out at the end of this year. I have a son who's eleven and he has a twelve-year-old friend who's a girl. We have a new book called *Chicken Soup for the Teenage Soul and the Tough Stuff.* It's all about dealing with parents' divorces, teachers who don't understand you, boyfriends who drink and drive, and other issues pertinent to that age group. I asked my son's friend, "Why do you like this book?" (It's our most popular book among teens right now.) She said, "You know, whenever I'm feeling down I read it and it makes me cry and I feel better. Some of the stories make me laugh and some of the stories make me feel more responsible for my life. But basically I just feel like I'm not alone."

One of the people I work with recently said that the books are like a support group between the covers of a book—you can read about other peoples' experiences and realize you're not the only one going through something.

**Wright**

Jack, with our *Speaking of Success* series we're trying to encourage people in our audience to be better, to live better, and be more fulfilled by reading about the experiences of our writers. Is there anyone or anything in your life that has made a difference for you and helped you to become a better person?

**Canfield**

Yes and we could do ten books just on that. I'm influenced by people all the time. If I were to go way back I'd have to say one of the key influences in my life was Jesse Jackson when he was still a minister in Chicago. I was teaching in an all black high school there and I went to Jesse Jackson's church with a friend one time. What happened for me was that I saw somebody with a vision. (This was before Martin Luther King was killed and Jesse was of the lieutenants in his organization.) I just saw people trying to make the world work better for a certain segment of the population. I was inspired by that kind of visionary belief that it's possible to make change.

Later on, John F. Kennedy was a hero of mine. I was very much inspired by him.

Another is a therapist by the name of Robert Resnick. He was my therapist for two years. He taught me a little formula called E + R = O that stands for Events + Response = Outcome. He said, "If you don't like your outcomes quit blaming the events and start changing your responses." One of his favorite phrases was, "If the grass on the other side of the fence looks greener, start watering your own lawn more."

I think he helped me get off any kind of self-pity I might have had because I had parents who were alcoholics. It would have been very easy to blame them for problems I might have had. They weren't very successful or rich; I was surrounded by people who were and I felt like, "God, what if I'd had parents like they had? I could have been a lot better." He just got me off that whole notion and made me realize the hand you were dealt is the hand you've got to play and take responsibility for who you are and quit complaining and blaming others and get on with your life. That was a turning point for me.

I'd say the last person who really affected me big time was a guy named W. Clement Stone who was a self-made multi-millionaire in Chicago. He taught me that success is not a four-letter word—it's nothing to be ashamed of—and you ought to go for it. He said, "The best thing you can do for the poor is not be one of them." Be a model for what it is to live a successful life. So I learned from him the principles of success and that's what I've been teaching now for more than thirty years.

### Wright

He was an entrepreneur in the insurance industry, wasn't he?

### Canfield

He was. He had combined insurance. When I worked for him he was worth 600 million dollars and that was before the dot.com millionaires came along in Silicon Valley. He just knew more about success. He was a good friend of Napoleon Hill (author of *Think and Grow Rich)* and he was a fabulous mentor. I really learned a lot from him.

## Wright

I miss some of the men I listened to when I was a young salesman coming up and he was one of them. Napoleon Hill was another one as was Dr. Peale. All of their writings made me who I am today. I'm glad I had that opportunity.

## Canfield

One speaker whose name you probably will remember, Charlie "Tremendous" Jones, says, "Who we are is a result of the books we read and the people we hang out with." I think that's so true and that's why I tell people, "If you want to have high self-esteem, hang out with people who have high self-esteem. If you want to be more spiritual, hang out with spiritual people." We're always telling our children, "Don't hang out with those kids." The reason we don't want them to is because we know how influential people are with each other. I think we need to give ourselves the same advice. Who are we hanging out with? We can hang out with them in books, cassette tapes, CDs, radio shows, and in person.

## Wright

One of my favorites was a fellow named Bill Gove from Florida. I talked with him about three or four years ago. He's retired now. His mind is still as quick as it ever was. I thought he was one of the greatest speakers I had ever heard.

What do you think makes up a great mentor? In other words, are there characteristics that mentors seem to have in common?

## Canfield

I think there are two obvious ones. I think mentors have to have the time to do it and the willingness to do it. I also think they need to be people who are doing something you want to do. W. Clement Stone used to tell me, "If you want to be rich, hang out with rich people. Watch what they do, eat what they eat, dress the way they dress. Try it on." He wasn't suggesting that you give up your authentic self, but he was pointing out that rich people probably have habits that you don't have and you should study them.

I always ask salespeople in an organization, "Who are the top two or three in your organization?" I tell them to start taking them out to lunch and dinner and for a drink and finding out what they do. Ask them, "What's your secret?" Nine times out of ten they'll be willing to tell you.

This goes back to what we said earlier about asking. I'll go into corporations and I'll say, "Who are the top ten people?" They'll all tell me and I'll say, "Did you ever ask them what they do different than you?"

"No," they'll reply.

"Why not?"

"Well, they might not want to tell me."

"How do you know? Did you ever ask them? All they can do is say no. You'll be no worse off than you are now."

So I think with mentors you just look at people who seem to be living the life you want to live and achieving the results you want to achieve.

What we say in our book is when that you approach a mentor they're probably busy and successful and so they haven't got a lot of time. Just ask, "Can I talk to you for ten minutes every month?" If I know it's only going to be ten minutes I'll probably say yes. The neat thing is if I like you I'll always give you more than ten minutes, but that ten minutes gets you in the door.

### Wright

In the future are there any more Jack Canfield books authored singularly?

### Canfield

One of my books includes the formula I mentioned earlier: E + R = O. I just felt I wanted to get that out there because every time I give a speech and I talk about that the whole room gets so quiet that you could hear a pin drop—I can tell people are really getting value. Then I'm going to do a series of books on the principles of success. I've got about 150 of them that I've identified over the years. I have a book down the road I want to do that's called *No More Put-Downs,* which is a book probably aimed mostly at parents, teacher and managers. There's a culture we have now of put-down humor. Whether it's *Married With Children* or *All in the Family,* there's that characteristic of macho put-down humor. There's research now showing how bad it is for kids' self-esteem when the coaches do it so I want to get that message out there as well.

### Wright

It's really not that funny, is it?

**Canfield**

No, we'll laugh it off because we don't want to look like we're a wimp but underneath we're hurt. The research now shows that you're better off breaking a child's bones than you are breaking their spirit. A bone will heal much more quickly than their emotional spirit will.

**Wright**

I remember recently reading a survey where people listed the top five people who had influenced them. I've tried it on a couple of groups at church and in other places. In my case, and in the survey, approximately three out of the top five are always teachers. I wonder if that's going to be the same in the next decade.

**Canfield**

I think that's probably because as children we're at our most formative years. We actually spend more time with our teachers than we do with our parents. Research shows that the average parent only interacts verbally with each of their children only about eight and a half minutes a day. Yet at school they're interacting with their teachers for anywhere from six to eight hours depending on how long the school day is, including coaches, chorus directors, etc.

I think that in almost everybody's life there's been that one teacher who loved him or her as a human being—an individual—not just one of the many students the teacher was supposed to fill full of History and English. That teacher believed in you and inspired you.

Les Brown is one of the great motivational speakers in the world. If it hadn't been for one teacher who said, "I think you can do more than be in a special ed. class. I think you're the one," he'd probably still be cutting grass in the median strip of the highways in Florida instead of being a $35,000-a-talk speaker.

**Wright**

I had a conversation one time with Les. He told me about this wonderful teacher who discovered Les was dyslexic. Everybody else called him dumb and this one lady just took him under her wing and had him tested. His entire life changed because of her interest in him.

**Canfield**

I'm on the board of advisors of the Dyslexic Awareness Resource Center here in Santa Barbara. The reason is because I taught high school with a lot of kids who were called at-risk—kids who would end up in gangs and so forth. What we found over and over was that about 78 percent of all the kids in the juvenile detention centers in Chicago were kids who had learning disabilities—primarily dyslexia—but there were others as well. They were never diagnosed and they weren't doing well in school so they'd drop out. As soon as a student drops out of school he or she becomes subject to the influence of gangs and other kinds of criminal and drug linked activities. If these kids had been diagnosed earlier we'd get rid of a large amount of the juvenile crime in America because there are a lot of really good programs that can teach dyslexics to read and excel in school.

### Wright

My wife is a teacher and she brings home stories that are heartbreaking about parents not being as concerned with their children as they used to be, or at least not as helpful as they used to be. Did you find that to be a problem when you were teaching?

### Canfield

It depends on what kind of district you're in. If it's a poor district the parents could be on drugs, alcoholics, and basically just not available. If you're in a really high rent district the parents not available because they're both working, coming home tired, they're jet-setters, or they're working late at the office because they're workaholics. Sometimes it just legitimately takes two paychecks to pay the rent anymore.

I find that the majority of parents care but often they don't know what to do. They don't know how to discipline their children. They don't know how to help them with their homework. They can't pass on skills that they never acquired themselves. Unfortunately, the trend tends to be like a chain letter. The people with the least amount of skills tend to have the most number of children. The other thing is that you get crack babies (infants born addicted to crack cocaine because of the mother's addiction). In Los Angeles one out of every ten babies born is a crack baby.

### Wright

That's unbelievable.

### Canfield

Yes and another statistic is that by the time 50 percent of the kids are twelve years old they have started experimenting with alcohol. I see a lot of that in the Bible belt. The problem is not the big city, urban designer drugs but alcoholism. Another thing you get, unfortunately, is a lot of let's call it familial violence—kids getting beat up, parents who drink and then explode—child abuse and sexual abuse. You see a lot of that.

## Wright

Most people are fascinated by these television shows about being a survivor. What has been the greatest comeback that you have made from adversity in your career or in your life?

## Canfield

You know it's funny, I don't think I've had a lot of major failures and setbacks where I had to start over. My life's been on an intentional curve. But I do have a lot of challenges. Mark and I are always setting goals that challenge us. We always say, "The purpose of setting a really big goal is not so that you can achieve it so much, but it's who you become in the process of achieving it." A friend of mine, Jim Rohn, says, "You want to set goals big enough so that in the process of achieving them you become someone worth being."

I think that to be a millionaire is nice but so what? People make the money and then they lose it. People get the big houses and then they burn down, or Silicon Valley goes belly up and all of a sudden they don't have a big house anymore. But who you became in the process of learning how to do that can never be taken away from you. So what we do is constantly put big challenges in front of us.

We have a book called *Chicken Soup for the Teacher's Soul.* (You'll have to make sure to get a copy for your wife.) I was a teacher and a teacher trainer for years. But because of the success of the *Chicken Soup* books I haven't been in the education world that much. I've got to go out and relearn how do I market to that world? I met with a Superintendent of Schools. I met with a guy named Jason Dorsey who's one of the number one consultants in the world in that area. I found out who has the best selling book in that area. I sat down with his wife for a day and talked about her marketing approaches.

I believe that if you face any kind of adversity, whether losing your job, your spouse dies, you get divorced, you're in an accident like Christopher Reeves and become paralyzed, or whatever, you simply do what you have to do. You find out who's already handled the problem and how did they've handled it. Then you get the support you need to get through it by their example. Whether it's a counselor in your church or you go on a retreat or you read the Bible, you do something that gives you the support you need to get to the other end.

You also have to know what the end is that you want to have. Do you want to be remarried? Do you just want to have a job and be a single mom? What is it? If you reach out and ask for support I think you'll get help. People really like to help other people. They're not always available because sometimes they're going through problems also; but there's always someone with a helping hand.

Often I think we let our pride get in the way. We let our stubbornness get in the way. We let our belief in how the world should be interfere and get in our way instead of dealing with how the world is. When we get that out of that way then we can start doing that which we need to do to get where we need to go.

## Wright

If you could have a platform and tell our audience something you feel that would help or encourage them, what would you say?

## Canfield

I'd say number one is to believe in yourself, believe in your dreams, and trust your feelings. I think too many people are trained wrong when they're little kids. For example, when kids are mad at their daddy they're told, "You're not mad at your Daddy."

They say, "Gee, I thought I was."

Or the kid says, "That's going to hurt," and the doctor says, "No it's not." Then they give you the shot and it hurts. They say, "See that didn't hurt, did it?" When that happened to you as a kid, you started to not trust yourself.

You may have asked your mom, "Are you upset?" and she says, "No," but she really was. So you stop learning to trust your perception.

I tell this story over and over. There are hundreds of people I've met who've come from upper class families where they make big incomes and the dad's a doctor. The kid wants to be a mechanic and work in an auto shop because that's what he loves. The family says, "That's beneath us. You can't do that." So the kid ends up being an anesthesiologist killing three people because he's not paying attention. What he really wants to do is tinker with cars. I tell people you've got to trust your own feelings, your own motivations, what turns you on, what you want to do, what makes you feel good, and quit worrying about what other people say, think, and want for you.

Decide what you want for yourself and then do what you need to do to go about getting it. It takes work.

I read a book a week minimum and at the end of the year I've read fifty-two books. We're talking about professional books—books on self-help, finances, psychology, parenting, and so forth. At the end of ten years I've read 520 books. That puts me in the top 1 percent of people knowing important information in this country. But most people are spending their time watching television.

When I went to work for W. Clement Stone, he told me, "I want you to cut out one hour a day of television."

"Okay," I said, "what do I do with it?"

"Read," he said.

He told me what kind of books to read. He said, "At the end of a year you'll have spent 365 hours reading. Divide that by a forty-hour work week and that's nine and a half weeks of education every year."

I thought, "Wow, that's two months." It was like going back to summer school.

As a result of his advice I have close to 8,000 books in my library. The reason I'm involved in this book project instead of someone else is that people like me, Jim Rohn, Les Brown, and you read a lot. We listen to tapes and we go to seminars. That's why we're the people with the information.

I always say that your raise becomes effective when you do. You'll become more effective as you gain more skills, more insight, and more knowledge.

## Wright

Jack, I have watched your career for over a decade and your accomplishments are just outstanding. But your humanitarian efforts are really what impress me. I think that you're doing great things not only in California, but all over the country.

## Canfield

It's true. In addition to all of the work we do, we pick one to three charities and we've given away over six million dollars in the last eight years, along with our publisher who matches every penny we give away. We've planted over a million trees in Yosemite National Park. We've bought hundreds of thousands of cataract operations in third world countries. We've contributed to the Red Cross, the Humane Society, and on it goes. It feels like a real blessing to be able to make that kind of a contribution to the world.

## Wright

Today we have been talking with Jack Canfield, founder and co-creator of the *Chicken Soup for the Soul* book series. As of 2006, there are sixty-five titles and eighty million copies in print in over thirty-seven <u>languages</u>.

## Canfield

The most recent book is *The Success Principles*. In it I share sixty-four principles that other people and I have utilized to achieve great levels of success.

In 2002 we published *Chicken Soup for the Soul of America.* It includes stories that grew out of 9/11 and is a real healing book for our nation. I would encourage readers to get a copy and share it with their families.

## Wright

I will stand in line to get one of those. Thank you so much being with us on *Speaking of Success.*

# About The Author

JACK CANFIELD is one of America's leading experts on developing self-esteem and peak performance. A dynamic and entertaining speaker, as well as a highly sought-after trainer, he has a wonderful ability to inform and inspire audiences toward developing their own human potential and personal effectiveness.

Jack Canfield is most well-known for the *Chicken Soup for the Soul* series, which he co-authored with Mark Victor Hansen, and for his audio programs about building high self-esteem. Jack is the founder of Self-Esteem Seminars, located in Santa Barbara, California, which trains entrepreneurs, educators, corporate leaders, and employees how to accelerate the achievement of their personal and professional goals. Jack is also the founder of The Foundation for Self Esteem, located in Culver City, California, which provides self-esteem resources and training to social workers, welfare recipients, and human resource professionals.

Jack graduated from Harvard in 1966, received his ME degree at the university of Massachusetts in 1973, and earned an Honorary Doctorate from the University of Santa Monica. He has been a high school and university teacher, a workshop facilitator, a psychotherapist, and a leading authority in the area of self-esteem and personal development.

As a result of his work with prisoners, welfare recipients, and inner-city youth, Jack was appointed by the state legislature to the California Task Force to Promote Self-Esteem and Personal and Social Responsibility. He also served on the board of trustees of the National Council for Self-Esteem.

Jack Canfield
Worldwide Headquarters
The Jack Canfield Companies
P.O. Box 30880
Santa Barbara, CA 93130
Phone: 805.563.2935
Fax: 805.563.2945
www.jackcanfield.com

# *Chapter 12*

## STEPHEN G. LIPSCOMB

THE INTERVIEW

**David Wright (Wright)**

Today we're talking with Stephen Lipscomb. He is a business consultant, avid golfer, and a professional member of the National Speakers Association. His expertise has driven him to focus on leadership development, selling strategies, and entrepreneurial development. Stephen has become addicted to the lessons that golf shows us about our lives. You might say he's golf-centric! He sees things from the greens that others obliviously walk and drive by.

Stephen works with progressive thinking and acting companies and individuals globally. He consults with Senior Teams, delivers powerful keynotes, and implements employee progression solutions.

He teaches men and women the power of doing business on the golf course. As he likes to say, "Human progress is like making your way around the golf course—it takes practice and patience and persistence!"

Stephen, welcome to *Speaking of Success.*

**Stephen Lipscomb (Lipscomb)**

Thank you, David!

**Wright**

I know you've heard many definitions of success, how do you define success?

**Lipscomb**

I think that a lot of times people look at success from the standpoint of what they have, how large their house is, what country club they belong to, what college they've attended, what style of Rolex are they are wearing—that sort of thing.

For me success has always been about what you have to offer and who have you become as an individual. Often people lose that perspective in their quest to be successful. Success is often related to someone being taken advantage of for another's personal gain. I think truly successful people put others' interests first and then look at how they can become better people. That is success because no matter where you go you are going to contribute something.

It's often mentioned that people have millionaire status because they are privileged. I believe that if you have millionaire mentality you will be a millionaire no matter where you go. If you're broke today, you can become a millionaire tomorrow. It's not just privilege; it's a mindset and a conditioning that we have to adhere to.

**Wright**

What would you say would be the biggest contribution to your professional success?

**Lipscomb**

I think it really goes back to childhood. I'm from Philadelphia, and being a Philly kid, things didn't come easy. We are all products of our environments; I just didn't believe that I had to be a victim of mine. I came from a divided household, so money was not in surplus by any means. When my mother would go shopping for me (I was about eleven) she would buy me the clothes that wouldn't wear out—clothes from Sears and Roebuck. They weren't the most fashionable clothes, so I'd get picked on and laughed at—I remember saying to my mom, "Hey, I would love to wear the types of clothes that the other kids in the neighborhood are wearing."

"Here's how much I'm spending," she would reply. "If you want to get those clothes or those sneakers, then you have to come up with the rest."

So I started very early learning how to make money in the neighborhood raking leaves, washing cars, shoveling snow—whatever I could do to make some money. And of course she got half of my earnings, so I would learn responsibility by a making a contribution to the household. So I would say that the biggest contribution was learning a solid work ethic that was instilled in me as a boy.

**Wright**

Aside from personal role models, who are the people who have served as your role models for success?

**Lipscomb**

David, there have been people I've met, and people I've never met and only have read about or listened to their audio programs or viewed their videos.

I think that some of the biggest role models are people in one's immediate life, like mothers, grandmothers, or other family members. Perhaps it could be a daughter or a wife. Then there are people like myself who become what could be considered as "people watchers." We watch the progress in others' lives. Perhaps our role models are spiritual leaders and how they apply Bible principals. My secular examples are: Jim Rohn, Zig Ziglar, Les Brown and Tony Robbins. The list goes on by—watching peoples' lives, their struggle and progress or their vicissitudes. I enjoy watching the athletes because I think that they are living a life very similar to being on stage as professional speakers; they have to perform for an audience.

It's a very lonely existence oftentimes being in our line of work, because we show up and then we go back to a lonely hotel or spend much time traveling from place to place.

So I think my role models include a lot of the greats out there, from reading the books they've written, listening to the seminars, and watching them in action.

**Wright**

What do you think are the biggest obstacles people face in trying to become successful?

**Lipscomb**

I think the biggest obstacle that people face is their own mindset, which oftentimes is contributed to by other people's opinions. Once a person sets out to do something, the pitfall that exists is it will be shared with everybody. Those with whom they share cannot help them to achieve their goals or success, so therefore others' opinions become their reality. For example, they might hear comments like, "We tried this before," or, "We did this before and it didn't work." "Who do you think you are? You're from this part of town," or, "Your skin color is this," or, "You don't have enough education to do such-and-such." I believe people become bogged down with the nay-sayers in their lives and those who have never really tried to do anything other than exist off the corporate dole or remain at the generation plant where a whole generation of family has worked. I believe that is the problem.

People need supportive environments to be successful, surrounding themselves with enough positive thinking and progressive people. Then they can share their goals with the people who can help them achieve them. If negativity sets in, the "stinking thinking" sets in, and as a result they are back doing what everyone else is doing, saying what everyone else is saying. They then have settled for being non-progressive in their lives.

**Wright**

How do you know what you need to be successful?

**Lipscomb**

You need to measure your success based upon your own abilities. If you're a carpenter today how realistic would it be to think that tomorrow you could be a cardiologist or something similarly outrageous? You have to be realistic. People say, "Use the power of positive thinking," and have a "positive mental attitude." That's true, but you need a level of realism as well. What are your skill sets? Look at what you have today—what do you offer? What do you like? What do you do well? Start there. I think the biggest thing people don't recognize is that success takes a period of time, and you build it in small chunks.

I remember I had the opportunity to meet the former heavyweight boxing champ Evander Holyfield. One of the things he said was that when he was training as a boy his trainer kept saying, "One day you'll to be the champ. I know you're going to the champ"—and then Evander said, "I didn't think it would take twenty years!" Sometimes people fool themselves into thinking that it's going to be an overnight thing, but nothing like success happens "overnight"! Everything is built upon something else and then we look back over a course of life and work history. That's where success comes from—by aligning yourself with what your attributes are, your passions, your physical wherewithal, a strong educational background, or whatever it is—align yourself with your strengths.

**Wright**

Would you tell our readers a little bit about what drives you to be successful?

**Lipscomb**

I think thankfulness—being thankful that I've had the opportunity to rise above mediocrity, and that started with a mindset and it keeps me motivated.

By knowing I have something to offer people that can benefit their lives, that adds to my drive to be successful. If they just hear one message that can start the process of change in their lives, then I would want to be a contributor to that!

Everything starts with self-discovery, which is the beginning of self-development. I believe that if I can help young people or professionals transition to a better place in their lives, then that's great. That's what keeps me going.

Jehovah God has gifted me with my attributes and my passion and my persuasiveness, so that's what keeps me trying to be better and do better. I'm never satisfied with what I have today, but I strive to become a better person each and every day.

**Wright**

Is it important to balance your success in your life? If so, how do you balance your success with your life?

**Lipscomb**

Life can get away from you, David, there's no question about it. When you're on the road 80 percent of the year doing domestic and international work like in Singapore or Europe, it gets rough. Anyone who says that it's "the glamorous life" also knows there's a lot of hard work that has to be put into it. You go from bad meals to bad hotel beds to noisy rooms to no ventilation. It is really not as glamorous as it appears to be sometimes. So when you have down time you must look at your health and your relationships. You also need to look at your nutrition and exercise.

You really have to find a way to balance it all out because the world and what you do for a living can take the last bit of energy right out of you, and balance is necessary. If you have children, take time to be with them. If you have a wife, take time to be with her. If you have other people in your family, you must take time to be with them because that makes you a stronger person to the audience and a stronger person to the commitment you make in the corporate world. It makes you a better you, and more powerful as a professional.

**Wright**

In the past you've spoken about passion being our compass for life and how it's the main factor in attaining success. Do you think that passion alone is enough?

**Lipscomb**

No, passion alone is not enough. It's almost like saying, "I can dream." However, a dream and a goal are two different things. A dream is something of a fantasy and a goal is something that you work at. And you realize that you achieve your dreams by virtue of working through goals and segments and chunks of life. Passion is something that keeps you in there; it keeps you coming back when you get knocked down. Here's a phrase from the well-known speaker, Les Brown: "If you can look up, you can get up." That has stayed with me over the years, because passion is what keeps you going—you have to have enough reasons why! And you must have some skill behind that passion.

You can be passionate about something; however, no one may want it. We need to be marketable and we need to be sure that we are offering people something they can use—something they can really benefit from. It's not just about profiting from something we are passionate about. It's others benefiting from something we are passionate about that they can take into their lives and that has value to them.

**Wright**

Les certainly walks his talk, he's been a friend for many years, but boy, I tell you, at one point in time when he had cancer, a lot of folks didn't know if he was going to come out of that or not.

**Lipscomb**

Yes, I'm familiar with that. We shared the platform a number of years back when he was just starting that whole process and it was very difficult for him. I'm glad to see that he's made much progress and is still making great things happen.

**Wright**

Why are more people not in tune with their passion if it's something all people possess?

**Lipscomb**

Again, I think it's a matter of "other peoples' opinions," it's a matter of tradition, and it's a matter of how failure is viewed. A lot of times people try things and fail. You can probably finish this quote, "Behind every successful man there is a . . ." What would you say, David?

**Wright**

"Woman."

**Lipscomb**

Okay, you say woman, that's also true. I'm going to say that behind every successful man is "a lot of failure"! The reason there is a lot of failure is because failure is something that takes place in order to find the "passion of success." Again, we go back to the reasons why a person does something that is closely related to the passion. And what happens with the failure is that people look at failure and they take it personally. They look at rejection, and take it personally. We have to understand that failure is an event, failure is not the person. When we recognize that, a person can then tune into his or her passions.

We also talk about "stinking thinking" and "rag mentality" and "brag mentality." Some people prefer to sit around and complain as opposed to actively doing something. "Rag mentality" is to blame the government, blame the administration, blame where you live, blame the water—they want to blame everyone and everything instead of looking in the mirror. And then the "brag mentality" sets in—"Oh, I'll buy this car," or "I'll join this country club, now I'm successful," but really often they're just in debt. That is what keeps people from tuning into their passion, it's called honesty. We need to be authentic.

When people become authentic they are then in a position to find their real selves within their passion.

## Wright

We all know what the dictionary definition of passion is, but how do you define it?

## Lipscomb

As I said earlier, the definition of success is defined by the phrase, "behind every successful man there is a lot of failure." I recall failing in my first marriage. After a very bitter ten-year relationship I was working in a commission-only job. I remember going forty-five days without receiving compensation. So I wasn't in the best place of my life financially at this point. When forty-five days went by someone said, "Why don't you just go and get a real job?"

I was a training consultant for a well-known organization—the Dale Carnegie organization—and I was doing some really great work with them. I knew that this was going to be the thing that was going to jump-start my career. To define "passion" is to do something that you would love to do without being paid for it, and I wasn't getting paid—I knew I would eventually get paid for it—so I hung in there. I soon broke a record for the largest six-figure sale the company had known at that time. That took care of my financial situation and I was back on the success track. I tell you, passion is defined for me as the answer to the question, "What would you do if you woke up tomorrow and money wasn't an issue?" And that, for me, is passion.

People who go to work for money first soon lose their passion. If you do what you like (passion) the money will come. People get that backwards. They go to work for the money instead of going to work for what they believe in and what makes them have a sense of purpose, progress, excitement, and fulfillment, which is motivation.

## Wright

How did you conclude that speaking was your passion?

## Lipscomb

David, people would tell me that I had presence and persuasion. I got into speaking from the sales and marketing side of things. I was making presentations and conducting sales and public speaking seminars. I would also make regular presentations at The Theocratic

Ministry School as a student. Then one thing led to another—Toastmasters and then the National Speakers Association.

**Wright**

You talked about people who influenced your life like Les Brown and Zig Ziglar. How can people help others succeed?

**Lipscomb**

We must become aware that people are constantly observing us. I go back to my old neighborhood; people often say that we are a product of our environment. I always say that we don't have to be victims of it. We can profit by our environments by virtue of understanding that people are listening to what we say; they are watching every move we make, and whether we accept it or not we *are all* an example and a role model. What will we chose to show them?

I'll give you one small example. The barber shop is the hub for most neighborhoods. As a rule men get together there and they talk as they get their haircuts, because it takes a while. I remember recently there were some young boys in the shop and the barber commented that their generation was lazy and hopeless. I asked him, "Why would you say something like that? Why would you condition their mindset; that their lives were hopeless? Subconsciously they will live up to that reputation, so why not give them a fine reputation to live up to? That negative projection will guide them until either they change environments or expand their thinking by other resources and experiences." (Unfortunately, that may never happen.)

We have to be careful about what we say because once we say it, it can never be taken back. That's one thing I would say—to be careful about what we put out there. Put positive messages out there! You can't measure success by saying that everyone's going to be at the same place. We are not all going to be at the same place. It doesn't mean that a carpenter who has a carpentry business is not successful. It doesn't mean that a landscaper who has a landscaping business is not successful. If you're not working in a lucrative position in a corporate ivory tower, that doesn't mean you're not successful.

We have to recognize that success is based upon giving the best of ourselves that we can give and making sure that our speech and our conduct is such that people say, "Wow! That person is really trying. That person is really setting a good example." That's what we can do to help other people.

**Wright**

Would you say that when people follow their passion, and excel at it, the passion brings success, or does success bring more passion?

**Lipscomb**

I think that when they follow their passion, passion is going to bring success, but we can't distort it. We have to recognize that we will have to start with small chunks and recognize what it is.

Some people actually speak for a living who have started out giving free speeches. Some of those same people are now getting paid hundreds of thousands of dollars to make presentations around the world. So yes, that will make you more passionate.

I think people need to be honest with themselves and understand that it's not an overnight thing. Many people have talked about overnight success and "getting rich quick." I believe that your passion does bring you more success if you recognize and remain thankful for everything you have, and not become greedy. As a result of that, yes, passion does bring more success and success more passion. But at first it's going to be a lot of hard work, with some disappointment along the way.

I remember back in 1995 saying that speaking was what I wanted to do for a living, and it's taken a good part of ten years to get where I am. I'm still not where I really want to be. I'm well along my way in doing what I love to do. If it takes twenty years, that's fine. If it takes thirty years, well, as a result of the experience from the journey, I would hope to have become better as a person from it.

**Wright**

What makes your perspective unique?

**Lipscomb**

I don't know that it's so unique, but for me it just appears to be a conditioning—a mental contract—there's "no growth in comfort" and "life is a choice." Find the solution, experience the highs and lows of life, "let it go," and keep it moving.

Some people may have careers with little disturbance. Most professionals in my field have come from corporate or educational positions to consulting and speaking. I didn't take the traditional track. I had to change my environment from a tough Philly kid to the military first, and then formal education. From there I transitioned to the corporate world. I started a few businesses along the way and I've had successes in my businesses and disappointments. I've had successes in corporate and disappointments. Each challenge and change has led to a new area of growth and opportunity.

I think that if anyone says he or she has had a challenge-free career, I'd wonder if that person is really being authentic. Honesty with self is what allows people to "grow through" things and helps them recognize their value. So I think being authentic is what makes a difference—that you've been there and have the battle scars and you're still willing to get up every day and say, "Let's do it again!"

### Wright

Tell me, what is the difference between a coach and a directional consultant? I understand that you are a directional consultant, is that right?

### Lipscomb

That's correct. The difference is that a coach is someone who is going to be in there with you by virtue of what you're currently doing. So we coach and we are helping people along the path they have already aligned themselves with. When you're looking at a directional consultant you're mapping out a place for them to go.

As an example, I was working with an executive from a Fortune 500 company. I saw that his leadership was not being respected. He had the title, but he didn't have the respect. When you don't have respect, things get done behind your back and over your head. I recommended that he think about and create an exit strategy.

If you don't have an exit strategy, someone may have one for you, and it may not be in your best interest. Then you're stuck at that point.

The suggestion I made was for him to use his educational background and his corporate experience in banking and financial services to start his own consulting practice and provide a service. He had a great educational "pedigree."

I suggested that he be a consultant because he was not very effective as a department leader. He was rather spineless and people walked all over him. I told him, "If you can't function in this environment, you might want to try functioning in a different environment where you make the rules. If you want to win at the game, sometimes you have to make your own rules!"

I continued to working with him for a solid four years. He had still not followed my recommendations. He just went from job to job. Often he's out of work. If he had followed my original recommendation he probably would be well on his way to making a very successful practice. He had something to offer, but he was not very effective in the role he had, so coaching him was doing very little for him. Sometimes you have to get a different direction, a different mindset, and a whole new environment for you to function and thrive in.

The challenging mindset is that people believe we all have strengths and weaknesses, that's the common thought. In my opinion we all have strengths and limitations. However, our limitations don't have to limit us. So if you have a limitation, you can either delegate the responsibility, take additional training, or just get rid of it altogether and take on something that is more in alignment with your strengths. That is the challenge, and that is where directional consultation comes into play.

**Wright**

What is the message you want people to hear so they can learn from your success?

**Lipscomb**

The message is that people really need to ask themselves, "What is it that I want to become?" more than "What can I get?" People think being a millionaire is all about the money. If you set a goal to become a millionaire, it's not so much the money you have, it's what you become as a result of going through that challenge of getting it. It's the ups and downs, the highs and lows, the fake-outs, and all the stuff that comes with business and success. And learning to read people and understand their intentions. I think it's really what you become. If people can just put that in perspective—to *become* more as opposed to *having* more—it's important because if you become more you'll get more!

You asked me earlier if passion follows success, and does success add to your passion. Yes, passion does feed on itself if you have your priorities aligned correctly.

Give more of yourself, help other people, become a mentor to someone, collaborate with someone who's just getting started in the business. Help people out as best you can. The more you give, the more you get. That's scriptural.

**Wright**

What an interesting conversation, Stephen. I really appreciate your taking all this time with me to answer all these questions. It's been enlightening and I've learned a lot.

**Lipscomb**

Thank you, I appreciate it, and I thank you for arranging this interview.

**Wright**

Today we've been talking with Stephen G. Lipscomb. He works with progressive thinking and acting companies and individuals globally. He consults with senior teams; delivers keynotes and implements employee progression solutions. Stephen is into training and playing golf—he teaches men and women the power of doing business on the golf course. As he says, "Human progress is like making your way around a golf course—it takes practice, patience, and persistence," and he's certainly convinced me of that today.

Stephen, thank you so much for being with on *Speaking of Success.*

**Lipscomb**

Thank you, David.

# About the Author

STEPHEN G. LIPSCOMB is a professional speaker and consultant with expertise in leadership, entrepreneurship, and selling strategies. Stephen has parlayed seventeen years of corporate sales and human relation experience into the creation of a premier training and development company. Since 1995, A.I.PLINC has focused on the development of leaders and managers in progressive organizations.

Formerly a training consultant and speaker for Dale Carnegie Training, Inc., Stephen validated his expertise by becoming certified to facilitate thirty professional development seminar programs. His proficiency in sales, marketing, and management has earned him several awards and accolades, an International Achievement Award, in addition to other regional awards. Stephen's expertise is internationally recognized in the areas of employee performance and organizational cultural change.

Progressively involved in personal, professional, and organizational development for the past thirteen years, Stephen's experience has served Technology, Pharmaceutical, Commercial Banking, Telecommunications, and Specialty Sales industries.

Stephen's voracious appetite for reading and learning spans numerous diverse subjects, including business, finance, biographies, psychology, health, and fitness. His desire for education and wisdom easily translates to generating fresh ideas that have become the signature for his consulting success.

Stephen believes it is important to give back to the community and serves on committees that benefit the neighborhood, youth, and those less fortunate. He frequently speaks to progressive college students and leads discussions on career development and employment marketability.

Stephen's personal philosophy, borrowed from his mentor Sam Iorio, is that "the short-cut to success is the long way." He believes that when a person stands up to speak, he or she should speak not to impress but to be understood.

Stephen G. Lipscomb
A.I.PLINC
SE Pennsylvania
Phone: 302.275.4624
E-mail: plinc@plincorg.com
www.plincorg.com
sgl@sprint.blackberry.net

# Chapter 13

## LAUREN BROWN-PERRY

### THE INTERVIEW

**David Wright (Wright)**

Today we're talking with Lauren Brown-Perry, JD. She teaches undergraduate courses in the Career Core and Criminal Justice Departments at Bryant & Stratton Business College in Milwaukee, Wisconsin. She previously taught at Herzing Career Technical College in Madison, Wisconsin, as well as the University of Wisconsin Madison Law School. Lauren is a consummate teacher and trainer, having trained business owners, corrections officials, and law enforcement executives on a variety of legal and management issues. Lauren has developed curriculum and training materials for a broad range of topics such as business law, trial advocacy, and community advocacy. She has trained many volunteers and community members on social justice and legal issues.

Lauren has advocated on behalf of low income, marginalized populations, and formerly incarcerated men and women while serving as a community coordinator for an interfaith social justice agency.

Lauren practiced law in Illinois and Wisconsin for over twenty years as a former deputy and assistant prosecutor, defense attorney, guardian *ad litem*, UW law professor, and attorney in private practice. She handled business, criminal, juvenile, and family matters, trying over one hundred cases in her extensive legal career.

Lauren credits her success with her faith in God and support of her husband, Martel, and their daughter, Ayilé, who is a student at a historically black college in Tennessee. Lauren values the love and support of her four sisters, her brother, and many nieces and nephews. "These are the keys to my success!" she says.

Lauren, welcome to *Speaking of Success.*

**Lauren Brown-Perry, JD (Brown-Perry)**
Thank you.

**Wright**
What is your definition of success and how do you measure it?

**Brown-Perry**
To me success means accomplishing what you set out to do, doing it well, and being satisfied with your accomplishment. I measure success by how I feel about my accomplishments and mostly how my accomplishments help others.

**Wright**
Do you have a motto?

**Brown-Perry**
I have something I remind myself of all the time: try, try, and never give up!

**Wright**
When we talked before you said there were at least ten elements of your success. Will you list and explain them for our readers?

**Brown-Perry**
First and foremost is faith. I believe that faith is what carries us through as individuals. I have a strong faith in God and a strong faith in people as individual human beings. Faith is what has carried me throughout my life. There have been times when I felt that if I didn't have faith I don't know where I'd be.

Motivation is one of the elements of my success—being motivated to do what it is I set out to do.

Determination is very important because you can get easily distracted or become disinterested in something that you're doing, no matter how much you want to do it.

Perseverance is very a much a part of being successful. Along with motivation and determination, perseverance gives you that ability to strive forward and keep going.

Dedication is also necessary to succeed. You have to be dedicated to what you want to do, again, because you can be easily distracted or taken off task.

You have to be a risk-taker to be successful, in my view, because success does involve stepping outside your comfort zone and outside of the box, so to speak, in pursuing excellence.

This leads me to excellence—excellence in what you're doing. You have to strive for and constantly achieve excellence. You keep raising the bar to excel in your excellence.

I believe one has to be selfless in what one is doing. By this I mean that whatever you do, first of all do no harm. This comes from the Hippocratic Oath that doctors take. At the same time you're there to help others. By helping others and feeling that satisfaction in helping them you are actually showing and feeling success yourself.

You have to have a desire to be successful. Something within you must help you strive to go forward—to encourage you to pick yourself up after you have setbacks.

Last but not least, I also think you have to have humility. Humbleness is something I work on every day. I think humility is very, very important to me in being successful.

**Wright**

Of all of these, which one or two do you think are the most important elements?

**Brown-Perry**

The most important one for me is faith. The other one I would say is humility.

**Wright**

Why would you say that?

**Brown-Perry**

For faith, it's the head of my life and what keeps me going. I think humility is important because you can get too full of yourself. I said earlier that one of my measures of success is being able to be selfless about it and to help others. Because of that you have to focus not so much on yourself but on how you can assist others.

Humility is hard for most of us, particularly people who are accomplished and who are very successful. I think humility is one of those characteristics that is a challenge. I know it is for me from time to time.

### Wright

It's been said that if you're walking down the road and you see a turtle sitting on a fencepost you can bet he didn't get up there by himself. So who are two of the most influential people in your life as far as your success is concerned? Who helped you "get on top of the fencepost"?

### Brown-Perry

I would say my parents—primarily my mother, who passed away some years ago. I'm the oldest of six children. She raised us for the most part by herself. She started college and then decided to get married and have a family. She attended college at a time when not many African American women were going to college. Even though she didn't finish, she instilled in us the desire to go to college. She was uncompromising in terms of education and so I thank her a lot for that.

The other person is a man who owned his own real estate business and who I worked for one summer. His name is Mr. Shelton. Mr. Shelton grew up in Chicago and came from modest means. He was a friend of our family and was always in business. He always treated people with respect. He was an excellent businessperson. I learned a lot about dealing with people, clients, and customers from him. He maintained humility throughout his business career.

I would say my mother and Mr. Shelton were the most influential people in my life as far as my success is concerned.

### Wright

In regard to your mother's uncompromising position on education, was she still alive when you received your doctorate of jurisprudence?

### Brown-Perry

Yes, she was. As a matter of fact, I had been practicing about nine years when she died. She was there when I received my license. I actually graduated early—I didn't graduate with my class, I received my JD in the mail before my class graduated and so I didn't go through the graduation ceremony. When I was admitted to the State of Illinois Bar, she attended the ceremony. She had a chance to see me grow and be successful in my legal career.

After my first year of law school, I found out that my mom's high school classmates had voted her most likely to be successful. Everyone thought she would be a lawyer. Even though she was very supportive of my choices and my career, she never told me about that until I was in law school, which I thought was interesting.

### Wright

Tell us about the parts of your background that contributed the most to your success.

### Brown-Perry

One is my humble beginning. I grew up in public housing in Chicago in the sixties. The turbulent sixties and seventies had a great influence on my ultimate success. Even though I had humble beginnings I spent time with businesspeople like Mr. Shelton. I was around people who were positively desirous of success not only for themselves but for us as kids growing up in our community. Both of my parents instilled success in us. My mother worked in some of the schools we attended. My dad had a middle school education. He highly valued education and was a stickler with us about that. Education was our ticket out of public housing and humble beginnings.

I'd say the Civil Rights Movement had an influence on me. I say that not because of the discontent and racial problems that were going on in the country, but because it was a time when a lot of folks were thriving and showing an entrepreneurial spirit. They were at their best in some ways during that time in our country.

I also appreciated being viewed as a competent individual, not just a female, not just an attorney, not just an African American person, but as a competent person in my field. I'm considered an expert in several areas of the law as a result of that. I was allowed to grow, develop, and make mistakes, ask questions, be supported, and valued all throughout my life by my family, educators, and those who had the most influence in my life. The support of my family and friends has been a valuable asset to me. I actually have seven close childhood friends. We are still friends who are accomplished, successful people in our own fields.

I was told "no" a lot. I heard, "You can't do this. You shouldn't try that." That was just an incentive for me to try harder. When people tell me no, part of me says, "Okay, this is a challenge; you're going to be ready for the challenge and you're going to show people they are wrong." Being told no actually contributed to my success. When I hear the word "no" now I consider it to be just another word; to me it means just try again and that's what I'll do.

**Wright**

Would you share one or two of your personal success stories?

**Brown-Perry**

One of the things that I am just so very proud of is having a supportive husband. All couples have their issues but my husband has been very supportive. I met him after I graduated from law school. He's seen me as a professional person, a career woman, an attorney, teacher, and trainer. I have known him all of my professional life. We have a daughter who is in college. She is majoring in hospital administration and she's going to pursue her MBA. I always tell her she's going to take care of her parents one day! That's also a personal success story—having a wonderful child who is a motivator in my life. My students can tell you that I talk about my daughter a lot. I check in regularly with her to be sure I'm using a generation-appropriate teaching approach with them.

Another success story concerns an outline for a book for a group of formerly incarcerated men and women. They call their group "Voices Beyond Bars." I wrote the outline about five years ago. Earlier this year, twenty men and women shared their stories about what their life was like during the first twenty-nine days after release from prison. That book is now published. I am so proud of that and I tell them, "This is just one of many because you can have the first sixty days, the first six months, the first couple of years, and so on." There are so many subsequent books they have the opportunity of doing. I am really thankful they were able to get that done. They are the only ones who can really tell their story. They've done it and the book is doing well.

**Wright**

Why did you pick those two stories to share with our readers?

### Brown-Perry

Because one is personal to me—I've produced a daughter who is doing well and is the light and love of my life. Family is very important to me and I believe that one measure of success is how much you give back.

Certainly you're going to give back to your family but how much do you give back to others you don't have a responsibility for or obligation to? That's also the reason why I picked the second story because there is a disproportionate number of African American men and women who are in the criminal justice and prison systems. I've learned a lot about myself and about our society by working closely with these men and women, most of whom are parents and married and who have families they do their best to support.

### Wright

Will you share a couple of business strategies that contributed to your success thus far?

### Brown-Perry

I think first and foremost you must be thoroughly prepared. You should know about the success journey you are on. If it's being an entrepreneur, you need to utilize all the tools available to you.

I have tried many cases over my legal career. I had to be thoroughly prepared for those cases. (By the way, I won most of the cases I tried both as a prosecutor and as a defense attorney.)

The second business strategy that I think has contributed to my success is that of perseverance and risk-taking. I use those terms together because I think they are that important. Risk-taking involves cutting-edge thinking, trailblazing, and being unconventional.

Another aspect is perseverance. Markets go up and down, clients and customers are not there all the time so you do have to persevere.

### Wright

Why do you say that you are still on this success journey?

### Brown-Perry

First of all, I would say that I don't think God is through with me yet. There's more He has in store for me to accomplish and to realize in life.

Looking at my journey so far, I know I have a lot of accomplishments but I feel that the greatest one is yet to come. I believe I'm still on this journey because I'm a life-long learner. I think there are always ways to improve. Even if you're at the top of your game, there is room for improvement. Being published as a college student is quite an accomplishment. I am looking forward to publishing more books and articles.

I have more to give back. I said earlier that one measure of success is how much you help others and how much you give back. I'm not through with that yet. I've been very blessed in my life and I want to share that blessing. By sharing your blessing you are blessed even more. So that's why I say I'm still on this journey.

### Wright

As you have made your decisions down through your career, has faith played an important role in that?

### Brown-Perry

It definitely has. I go to the Master first and ask for direction and pray on it. I know that if I do my best and He is at the helm, everything is right with the world. I have faith that all will turn out. Things turn out one way or another but things turn out the best when you take the proper approach. I believe that if you have faith you can do anything. I am a living testimony.

In college, I read a report about the public housing project I grew up in. At that time, Robert Taylor Homes was the largest housing project in the world. It doesn't exist anymore. The report was dismal and it contained so many negative statistics about where I grew up. That wasn't my experience. Frankly, if I had believed that report, I probably wouldn't be where I am today!

Faith is really important. I know that my faith can overcome my circumstances. That was a real challenge because it was like telling me "no" and I was not going to amount to anything in life. I grew up with a number of people for whom that is true; but I knew it wasn't true for me. My parents told us that we may be living in the projects but it was not our end destiny.

I believe every generation needs to do better than the previous one, that's why I'm expecting so much from my daughter and her generation to accomplish so many more things than my generation was able to do.

**Wright**

As you consider the young people of today, what advice or suggestions would you give to aid in reaching their success?

**Brown-Perry**

I think they need to stay true to themselves. They are subject to a lot of peer influence. Depending on who your peer group is or who you more readily identify with, it can stunt your dreams and your fantasies and the goals you set. So stay true to yourself.

I say this to the students in my college classes who are in the age range of seventeen to twenty-five—do not give up. I tell them that they can accomplish anything they want to accomplish. First of all you have to dream and I even say fantasize about it—you have to visualize it for yourself. Then you have to make a decision about what it is you want to do and develop a plan of action. You are setting goals and implementing that plan—you're preparing yourself.

It's one thing to say you want to be a doctor when you grow up. It is another thing to determine that because you want to be a doctor, you're going to get used to reading, developing good study habits, and looking into the field of medicine. There are so many different specialties from which to choose. You have to associate with people in that field and ask questions and learn all you need to know about it. Then you have to believe you can do it. You have to see yourself at the end of that journey actually becoming a doctor. Then you have to excel so you will receive that satisfaction and then you have to give back—help others. As opportunities were made available to you, you have to help create them for others.

I also tell them to smile because it takes more muscles to frown than it does to smile. When they get my age they'll be glad that they smiled a lot. I also tell them to have fun. What's life without fun?

**Wright**

I appreciate all the time you've taken with me today to answer all these questions. I've certainly learned a lot. I wish you well. It seems that you're doing some great work and you have done some great work throughout your life.

Today we've been talking with Lauren Brown-Perry. She teaches undergraduate courses in the Career Core and Criminal Justice Departments at Bryant & Stratton Business College in Milwaukee. She has advocated on behalf of low income, marginalized populations, and formerly incarcerated men and women while serving as a community coordinator for an interfaith social justice agency. She actually walks her talk—she does what she says and she says we ought to help others. I don't know about you, but I believe her.

Thank you so much for being with us today, Lauren, on *Speaking of Success.*

# About the Author

LAUREN BROWN-PERRY, JD, teaches undergraduate courses in the Career Core, and Criminal Justice Departments at Bryant & Stratton Business College in Milwaukee, Wisconsin. She previously taught at Herzing Career Technical College in Madison, Wisconsin, as well as the University of Wisconsin Madison Law School. Lauren is a consummate teacher and trainer, having trained business owners, corrections officials, and law enforcement executives on a variety of legal and management issues. Lauren has developed curriculum and training materials for a broad range of topics such as business law, trial advocacy, and community advocacy. She has trained many volunteers and community members on social justice and legal issues.

Lauren has advocated on behalf of low income, marginalized populations, and formerly incarcerated men and women, while serving as a community coordinator for an interfaith social justice agency.

Lauren practiced law in Illinois and Wisconsin for over twenty years, as a former deputy and assistant prosecutor, defense attorney, guardian *ad litem,* UW law professor, and attorney in private practice. She handled business, criminal, juvenile, and family matters, trying over 100 cases in her extensive legal career.

Lauren credits her success to her faith in God and the support of her husband Martel and their daughter, Ayilé, who is student at a historically black college in Tennessee. Lauren values the love and support of her four sisters, her brother, and many nieces and nephews. She says, "These are the keys to my success!"

**Lauren Brown-Perry, JD**
1028 E. Juneau Avenue #724
Milwaukee, WI 53202
Phone: 414.469.9281
E-mail: lauren_brownperry@yahoo.com

# Chapter 14

### ALEX ZOLTAN SZINEGH

## THE INTERVIEW

### David Wright (Wright)

Today we're talking with Alex Zoltan Szinegh. He is Senior Regional VP for North America, Exit Realty Corporation International. Alex is a true "rags to riches" story. Armed with only a tenth grade education, this immigrant from Hungary has surmounted all odds to become an internationally recognized speaker, trainer, and performance coach. Alex has personally sold over 2,300 properties; he has run successful businesses, trained thousands of people in the art of "street smarts" and "how to succeed in spite of your circumstances and past." Alex is refreshing, funny, educational, and positively "in your face" with a candid style. He tells it like it is. Alex is a family man with four children, ages thirty-six, thirty-two, twenty-nine, and a four-year old. He also has five grandchildren. Alex's main drive to succeed in life has been his family, and his biggest supporter and inspiration is his wife, Cindy.

Alex, welcome to *Speaking of Success.*

So, what is your definition of "success"?

## Alex Zoltan Szinegh (Szinegh)

You know, it is so interesting—over the years people have asked me what my interpretation of "success" is. Going back to my early days and getting out into the workforce, I would have thought that "success" meant I make a certain amount of money, or I achieve a certain level, or I get a certain title, or I acquire material possessions. As the saying goes, "The guy with the most toys wins." I always thought that success was measured by things and status. As I journeyed through different jobs I gained a lot of education. I held many really great jobs and "success" became something different every time. Success started to become more of a vision, more of a lifestyle, more of an attitude than material possessions.

In my training and my coaching with people I talk about the wheel of life. I talk about all the different parts of life—spiritual, family, physical, mental, financial, fun, and business. I think true success, in my opinion, is the ability to balance the different parts of your life in such a way that you're comfortable with yourself, your surroundings, and the people around you. That's what success is—the ability to balance, to be able to achieve whatever you set your mind to, and make the decision that this is where you want to be, that you've arrived at that position.

When I say "arrived" at that position, I don't think we ever arrive at success, it's more of a flow, it's something that's always fluid, it is a journey more than a destination.

My first job out of school (I quit school in the eleventh grade) was in a factory; I was making $47.50 a week. I remember my boss coming to me and said, "Alex, we're going to give you a raise," and the company gave me a $2.50 a week raise. I always thought that once I made $50 a week I would be "successful" and I could go and buy a car. My first car cost $45. I know I'm dating myself but it was amazing and the car actually ran, so I thought that at fifty bucks per week, "I'm a great success."

Over the years I kept thinking that way. I thought, "If I make ten grand a year I'm a success. If I make a hundred grand a year—" Then I thought, "Well, once you make your first million you're a success—I always wanted to be a millionaire." But when you lose it all, then you think, "Maybe this isn't success." The biggest drive for me is family. I believe that having a good family life, being healthy, and just enjoying what you're doing is important. I think you can really truly call yourself a success if you happen to find the thing that you are really passionate about, love it, and be able to do it; that is when everything falls into place.

**Wright**

So if I understand you correctly, you're saying that success to you is a journey rather than a destination?

**Szinegh**

Absolutely. I didn't want to use that cliché, but I've watched a lot of great speakers—Jim Rohn, Tony Robbins, Robert Kiyosaki—I've read many, many books, listened to tapes, and I've attend many seminars. It seems that all of these people who are really successful talk a lot about the whole aspect of the journey. Unfortunately, we discover that too late in life. If we discovered it a little bit earlier I think we'd all be a lot better off. I think teaching goal-setting and more life skills on how to become successful would help a lot if it was taught in the earlier years of schooling.

**Wright**

How do you know when you are successful?

**Szinegh**

I can only think of one word, it's called "peace" with yourself—you have peace inside yourself. There was a survey done and it was discovered that people would rather die than be a public speaker, for example. You are successful when you are not afraid of anything in life and you're content with your position in life. You have the goals and desires to grow and get better, but you have arrived at a position where you have achieved a happy balance in every part of life—physically, mentally, emotionally, financially, spiritually, family, and in business. You have this feeling of euphoria that life is great and every day is great, and every moment is great. I think, for me, that's what it feels like.

**Wright**

What do you think it takes to become successful?

**Szinegh**

There are many different opinions about that. I think a lot of people believe they can take a course or a seminar and once they follow some step-by-step process they will become successful. I feel the process really starts when you find your passion.

Success is the journey, it's the process, it's that feeling versus the actual belief that one has arrived in a particular position. I think it's a never-ending, changing, shifting, drifting, moving target. I heard this at a seminar, "Set your goals as high as you want, as far as you can see, and when you get there you're going to notice that you can see farther." I've seen people doing demonstrations where they say, "Stretch your arm as far as you can," and you stretch and stretch and they'll ask if you're at the limit that you can stretch it and the audience says, "Yes!" Then they say, "Give me another quarter inch," and then the people stretch even farther. And there you are—you can go another quarter inch, you can stretch *farther*—you can definitely go farther.

I think one of the biggest killers of success today in our society is complacency. It's "settling" for only so much in your life all around you in all the different categories; it's "giving up." I heard a speaker say that the opposite of success is not fear, it's complacency. People get complacent, they "settle," they give up, they put their dream aside. I talk to people who are overweight and they make statements like, "I'm big-boned, it's in my genes, my family was always this way." If they don't have any money, they say, "Well, we were never rich, so we understood that it's okay for us not to be successful." I think one of the biggest misconceptions is when people quote the Scriptures and they say, "You know, it says right in the Bible that money is evil." Not true. What it says is that *the love of money* is evil (1 Timothy 6:10). It says right in the Bible that you are supposed to be rich (3 John 1:2), you have a responsibility to become rich—that is the only way you can help others.

In my training sessions I talk about this and sometimes people say, "You know what, I think what we need to do is we need to serve society, we need to help people, and we need to help the poor." My opinion is if you want to help the poor, step number one is *don't join them!* You can't do a lot of good if you haven't taken care of yourself.

I fly almost every week. Before the plane leaves the ground the flight attendant will say, "In the event of the loss of oxygen an oxygen mask will drop from the ceiling. If you're traveling with a child, you put yours on *first*." In other words, if you can't take care of you, you can't take care of anybody!

I think that's where we are in our society—we settle for too little, and we settle for less than we can be. And when we do that, we not only hurt ourselves, but we hurt all those people around us who trust us and count on us—those we are responsible for and whom we could give to.

I see it in my own family. I have three brothers. My older brother is brilliant. He has a college education and he's smart. Over the years I've watched him and he could have been a lot more successful if he had put a little more effort in certain areas, but he never chose to do that. He "settled." I see people in my training programs who "settle." They say, "Well, I just want this much. I don't want to go too far because if I get too rich or I get too successful I'll lose all my friends." We hold each other back sometimes.

The bottom line is this: find something you really love to do (something you can get passionate about), start doing it, continue to learn about it. Get extra training (you could even get a coach), dedicate your life to it, and success in all parts of your life will be virtually guaranteed.

**Wright**

Do you feel not having a formal education has slowed you down?

**Szinegh**

I don't think so. I really truly don't. It's not that I'm against education, I'm not against education, but I'm for a specific type of education. I think there are missing elements in schooling and teaching. I wish there had been somebody smart enough among my teachers and my professors and people who were teaching me along the way who knew about, for example, personalities and DISC behavior profiles tests. I also think I would have been a lot better off if, when I was in grade five and grade six and even grade one, somebody had taught me the value of money. But educators are not trained to do that. I wish that somebody had placed more of an emphasis on health and had said, "This is what you need to do to become healthy."

I believe that what we need to do is take the wheel of life to children. We need to show them the wheel of life and we need to show them that if they want to be successful in life, if they want to excel, it's not when they get straight A's or straight B's or whatever—it's got nothing to do with academic knowledge.

I believe that some of the things we desperately need training in early in life include: goal-setting, planning, specific skill development, and better time management.

As I was sitting in school when I was in grade seven and eight, I used to think to myself, "Why on earth do I need to know algebra? What benefit will I get out of knowing what the capital of Turkey is?" Why do I need to know this stuff? When I really thought about it, I realized that there was so much stuff put into my brain that was irrelevant to my life. I discovered more and more, as I started to read books, attend seminars, and listened to great speakers, that all of that stuff was just "stuff"! Unfortunately, our school system and our educational system are not designed to teach us all of the practical things of life.

You know, David, you've been in the Real Estate business and you know as well as I do that when somebody gets a real estate license, they may be called a real estate agent because they passed the test, but they sure as heck don't know how to sell real estate or how to deal with people, do they? The "real" training starts after they get a real estate license.

**Wright**

Right.

**Szinegh**

They only learn enough to pass the test, and I think that's a shame in our society. And here's another thing I think is a big problem about education: we are punished and we are kept being told what we "don't know" and what we do *wrong* as opposed to saying, "Oh, you've got all these things right! It seems to me, Alex, that you are leaning toward these kinds of things in your life. Why don't we enhance that and why don't we spend more time at what you're good at, versus beating you up with what you're not good at?"

When I was at an event this weekend, most of the speakers talked about how one can make it on one's own. In my life I would never have gotten as far as I did unless there had been other people who supported me or helped me. We call that "team effort" or "team work"—working together and building a relationship. In school you're never taught that. What are you taught? Early in life we are trained to *compete*. "Why can't you be like your big brother Johnny? Why do you do that? Why can't you do better in school? Your brother got better marks," so you're always competing in a win/lose situation—we're not trained to work as a team.

I presented this speech to a very large audience a couple of weeks ago on teamwork. It was interesting—my boss, Steve Morris, said to me, "I want you to speak about teamwork."

I started to think about my life, and I thought I was never a great team player because I thought about sports immediately. I always did individual sports—gymnastics, running, wrestling, one person against another, or me against myself. We were trained and conditioned to the win/lose mindset. I thought about teamwork and that a person is a team member in his or her family. I realized I had to look into this and start thinking about it. I even thought about school—if you want to practice teamwork how could you do that in a test? The concept of "teamwork" would involve your looking to your neighbor and saying, "I'm not sure about this answer. Would you help me with it?" That wouldn't be teamwork, it's cheating—you would get punished!

So in school you're not trained to work as a team, you're not trained to work in cohesion with other people. I think our education system needs improvement. All my kids finished schooling through grade twelve, so they all received more education than I did.

The best example is my oldest daughter, Michelle, who went to college. She lived at home and for years she watched me fail and succeed, fail and succeed, and go broke and lose money and make money, and succeed in business and fail again. During those years I'd be encouraging her and the rest of my children to read books like *Think and Grow Rich* by Napoleon Hill. I was trying to educate my children about success and about life.

Michelle went to college because she said she wanted to learn to become better. She enrolled and chose as her major business administration. She was in college for a couple of months when she came home and said, "Dad, my professor is telling me all the same things that you've been telling me."

"Why don't you ask your teacher how many businesses he has owned and operated?" I asked.

So she asked him, and she discovered that he had never run a business! He was somebody teaching my daughter how to become a success in business and he had *never* run a business!

I just got a pilot's license not too long ago. I was flying with this gentleman who was seventy-five years old. He had specific knowledge as a flight instructor. He would have scared the pants off me if I'd had to fly with him if he had only had book knowledge versus actual flight experience. But because he had actual experience, I trusted him—I felt safe. He did maneuvers with the little plane that were incredible, that scared me; but at the same time I felt very secure and safe that he could do it. And I think actual experience is what we don't learn in school. Sometimes we are taught by people who have a lot of "book learned" experience versus real life experience.

**Wright**

If you had to do it all over again what would you change?

**Szinegh**

Well, first of all, if I could do it all over again, looking back over the decisions I've made and the things that I've done, I think what I would do is definitely listen to my gut—my instincts—a lot more because over the years I missed a lot of opportunities. My gut feelings said I should do it, and I didn't go for it, and other times my gut says don't do it and my head or my heart said do it or greed said do it and I lost money and I got hurt and things happened. So I think the first thing I would do is listen to my gut instinct more.

The other thing I would do is I would definitely have gotten more education in specific areas. I would focus and make a decision about what I wanted to do with my life. I should have set my goals earlier, I should have read more books, and I should have followed more successful people. I should have taken coaching earlier in my life. I should have listened to people—not people with a bunch of degrees and a bunch of initials after their names—I would have listened to people who were in positions where I wanted to be. I wish I had awakened earlier in my life. I wish I had gotten smarter earlier.

I had parents who were average, middle-class folks. My father was just a regular working man working from paycheck to paycheck. My mother had a certain philosophy of money. I programmed myself according to their standards and their thinking. It took me twenty to thirty years to undo some of the programming I had acquired during my life at home.

I love everything about my life—I love the failures *and* the successes, because that's what got me here. When a great man was asked, "What do you think about the obstacles in your life? You had so many problems in your life," I heard him reply, "I used those obstacles as stepping stones to get me where I want to be." I think that's what happened with me. But if I could do it all over again, I would pay more attention. I would open up my eyes more, but unfortunately I did not have the role models back then.

I would definitely go for more specific training and knowledge, and it would be nice if more specific training was available in our school system today such as teaching people about the various personalities and how to get along with others.

I got married very early. I got married when I was nineteen years old and I became a father at twenty. It took me probably twenty years to figure out how to be a father. You go to a department store and you buy a toaster and it comes with instructions. But when you become a father, there's no instruction manual that comes with the kids. When you bring the baby home from the hospital you have to learn how give infant care by doing it. That's the educational process of understanding about how to grow and how to develop.

I used to think I was a terrible father. I wasn't a terrible father—I was just a certain type of personality. I have four children, and all four children are different personalities—very specifically different. I look at them now and I think, "I know why they did that." But back then I didn't know. So, being a certain personality type, and as a father, I thought that everybody should be like *me*, and I treated my children that way.

I think that's the reason I failed in business so often. The golden rule says, "Do unto others as you want it done to you." I kept doing that to others and it doesn't work—everybody is different.

I wish I had taken more people skill training and learned more about understanding others because it's through others that we grow. So if I could do it all over again, if I had the brain power back then that I've got today, who knows where I would be now! But you know what? I'm very happy where I am. I am very satisfied with where I am, and I know where I'm going and I'm excited about my life.

"I've gone through one marriage that didn't work because I didn't understand my spouse. I didn't understand her personality. People say to me, "It sounds as if it was tough and you must wish you had never married her." No, I don't wish I hadn't married her—she's a terrific woman; with her I have three wonderful children and now I have five grandchildren. I am actually thankful to her for the experiences and the lessons she taught me. Every experience was added to the next one—every experience is built on the one before it.

## Wright

For a guy your age you seem to have a lot of energy, so would you tell our readers what makes you go?

## Szinegh

I think the biggest thing that makes me go is being excited about life. A lot of people ask me, "Don't you ever get down?" When I look back at my life, twenty or thirty years ago I used to really get unhappy. I would be depressed for months sometimes. I'd go out drinking and partying as a diversion.

I'd also smoke. Then as I saw people around me—my father died of cancer, my wife's father died of cancer—I'd see people get sick around me, so I decided to quit smoking.

I knew that my mindset had to do with attitude. So I began to read books. What really got me excited was the very first motivational book I ever read. It was *Think and Grow Rich* by Napoleon Hill. I saw that there was hope for everybody! What excited me, and what really built this energy into me, was the opportunity and the understanding I gained that I have total control over my life. I *do* have control.

I know there are people who are going to say, "Wait a minute. God controls our life, we were put here." But I don't think that God put idiots on the earth. I think we are given a brain so that we can think for ourselves, and we can direct and control our life. That's exciting! It's exciting to me to get up in the morning and have a focus and know that I'm going someplace and doing something that I really love and have a passion about.

I think passion drives people, and the problem today is that people don't have the energy and don't have the passion. Most people hate their jobs, they're just in a job—they only do enough work so they don't get fired. They only get enough pay so that they don't quit. People are just not passionate about life. They are not passionate about their marriage, they are not passionate with the way they live, and they feel trapped. They feel that they don't have the option or an opportunity to move ahead or have total control over their life.

I saw a perfect example of that this morning, and I'm going to use this in my training today. I was having breakfast in the hotel. I had finished working out and there was a lady with two little children who were about four or five. As they walked in, they got their breakfast from the buffet and the lady put the plate and the orange juice and everything down on one of the tables. One little girl sat where this lady told her to sit and the other little girl sat at another table. The lady said to her, "No, honey, I want you to sit over here."

The little girl said, "No, I like this table and this is where I want to sit."

"No, no, honey, this is where we are going to sit."

I was watching this tug-of-war between the woman and the child. Within two minutes the lady, the plates, and everything went over to the other table, and this four- or five-year-old child was in full of control of the situation. She had said, "This is where I'm going to sit and this is where I am going to be," and she moved this adult person over! I was *amazed* just watching it.

There are so many people who think they have no control in life because they don't *ask* for it. That's where I think I get my energy from—it is the knowledge that I do have control. I can make a difference. I *can* make a change. I love what I do.

The other thing that I do (and I talk with people about this all the time) is that I exercise on a regular basis. Energy creates energy! This morning I was running on the treadmill. I didn't take long— probably twenty to twenty-five minutes. Exercise like that pumps your blood and gets you going. I don't understand all the physiological details but I do know that exercise creates endorphins in the body and chemical reactions that make you feel good. It's all about life!

Last night before I went to bed I spoke to my little girl over the telephone. It made me feel good to talk with her. All these things around me opened my eyes. Over the years I have become in awe of the little things. It's almost like I have more energy now.

I'm fifty-seven and every day I want to do as many push-ups as the number of years I've lived. This morning I thought, "I can do better." So this morning, in forty-five seconds I knocked off seventy push-ups! I thought, "That's not bad for an old guy!" It's the "excitement" that I felt that I could stretch and do *more*! Challenges like that keep me going and give me the energy.

I joined Exit when there were two offices and about fifty agents. Now we have a thousand offices and over 30,000 agents! I helped build that, and that gives me excitement.

I don't know who said it, but in one of the trainings I attended someone said, "If you give it away, you get more of it." I think that is one of the things that gets me energized and charged up—when I give it away. When I do a training or when I do a seminar—when I give something to somebody else—it just charges me right up. I'm like the Energizer bunny that just keeps going and going. I think that's where it comes from—it comes from different parts of my life.

Wright

Your company Exit is growing at a rapid pace. What makes your company so unique?

## Szinegh

This is absolutely incredible—I met the founder of Exit by accident. I've been in the real estate business for twenty-three years. There's no security in most jobs today, is there? Jobs are getting downsized, companies are closing, pension programs are going down the drain, and executives are stealing other people's money. Look at Enron—there's no future and no security.

Steve Morris, the founder of Exit, has been in the Real Estate business for many years. He said, "We have these huge problems in Real Estate and one of them is that it takes so long to get paid. Another problem is you can't stop; you cannot stop in this business. Once you get on it, it's like running on a treadmill. If you stop on a treadmill you fall flat on your face. Real Estate feels like that—you've got to keep going and keep selling and waiting for the next commission check. There's no wisdom passed down—nobody's going to help you because it's a competitive business. Everybody's competing against everybody else."

What Steve Morris did is look at the problems in real estate that have plagued the industry for fifty years.

He always said that agents are a very important asset to the business. Most corporation owners make a huge mistake of thinking it's their idea, it's their equipment, it's their product, it's their office building, it's all the money they have in the bank. They think all those things are their assets. I feel a lot of corporations think that as long as they have a good idea and something that looks good, that that's what makes the corporation. Steve believes passionately, and transposes this to all of his people, his executives, his brokers, and every salesperson, that *they* are the assets of the corporation! He said, "Why don't we pay tribute to the assets that we *have?*" So he built a system of rewarding people for helping him grow the corporation. Give them a piece of the action.

I've worked for many different corporations—huge Real Estate corporations—and their attitude was, "Give me your money every month, pay your bills, and don't bother me." But Steve believes that if you help the corporation to grow, he rewards you.

His program is called a "Single Level Residuals." That means if I bring someone into the corporation, the company rewards me for bringing that person from another company. That's how it works at Exit.

When I first joined the company I thought, "Oh yeah. Okay, if this thing ever works I'd be surprised." But it was amazing how quickly it started to catch on and Exit started to grow.

Can you imagine if you have an office of five agents and each of them brings one, and then next month each of them brings in one again? The growth and the compounding of numbers is phenomenal! So the company believes in rewarding its people.

The other thing is education. The biggest problem in the real estate business is lack of education. As I said before, the business is so competitive that most realtors do not want to mentor people who are new in the business.

In Exit we have systems in place that will build and rebuild and educate and push forward all of the agents in the company.

One of the most significant components that has driven this corporation is Steve's philosophy of passion about the company, about its people, and his ability to pass on this excitement. Steve practices affirmations. He does eight to ten pages of affirmations every morning and he's been doing it for maybe twenty-five or thirty years. Here's his method in his own words, "Write down what you want to happen that day. Write down your future and talk about what you want to take place." He projects this and he passes it on to his people.

He demonstrates just incredible leadership. I think that's what grows the corporation. That's also what grows a family—"leadership." A leader is somebody who has followers. If nobody's following you you're just taking a walk!

To this point, the company's success has been basically the passion, the incredible focus, and excitement. I think that's what drives it. You look around today—what corporations have passion? I think we lose that human factor and the company's employees become just numbers—they become statistics—they're not as important as they should be.

I think what makes our company so unique is that those who work here feel *important*—every single one of us. There's another system Steve put in place. Every agent pays a very small franchise fee, which is much smaller than most of the other real estate franchises. From that fee we take a little bit of money—only $5—and we put it toward Habitat for Humanity, the organization that builds houses for people who can't afford to have them. And what's amazing is, those tiny little $5 contributions have so far amounted to over $865,000 in donations to Habitat for Humanity!

Even the secretaries benefit. We take $5 out of every transaction and we put it into a secretarial fund. At the end of the year, based upon the seniority of the person and who worked there, and based on their hours and other factors, the secretaries in every office get a bonus. Now tell me, how many companies take part of their earnings and give it back to the secretaries? So every part of the organization is *giving*, which creates cohesion. I think that's what drives the company and that's what makes it so successful! What we say at Exit is, "It's real estate re-invented."

**Wright**

What is your advice to someone who is struggling to succeed?

**Szinegh**

The first thing is, recognize that you're struggling.

Jim Rohn has been my mentor over the years and he doesn't even know it. I've listened to him, I've watched him, I've personally met him several times, I've read his books, and I listen to his tapes. He says there's a day that turns your life around. He talks about many days, but he says that there's a particular day—he calls it the day of disgust—when you actually become disgusted about where you are. You've actually discovered you're struggling and you've actually understood you're in a hole. So stop digging!

When you undergo the revelation that you're struggling, step number one is to make that decision that you *are* struggling.

Step number two is to make the decision and understand that you *can* make a difference—you can *change*. If you change, your results will change.

Then what you need to do is to seek out people who are in positions you want!

There are two ways to learn in life: one is to make your own mistakes, and the other is to learn from the mistakes of others. Some of us couldn't live long enough to make all the mistakes, so we need to find role models—it's all about modeling. A lot of people don't understand that. We never learned about that in school.

I mentioned earlier I got my pilot's license to fly these little ultralight airplanes. My teacher has flown since he was fifteen years old. He was seventy-five years old when I was his student. He had been flying for sixty years. He has trained over 6,000 pilots without a single accident. So I knew he had the expertise and qualifications to teach me.

That's what people need to do. People need to seek out individuals who have the skills and knowledge to teach others about their field of expertise. People also have to be teachable and coachable. I think most of our society wants "instant this" and "instant that." We go to the drive-throughs and we want instant coffee.

I was reading in a magazine a few days ago that there's a place where quickie divorces can be done. There are other places where they hold five-minute dating. Relationships change very quickly; people are not putting any emphasis on relationships.

What people have to do is realize they're struggling and then seek out somebody who is doing better, somebody who can help them.

I went to a gym one time and the guy behind the counter was probably fifty pounds overweight! I thought, *"Hello!* Look at the equipment! Look around you!"* You've probably heard this saying "Never go to a bald barber."

There's lots of help available out there. People who are reading this book really need to understand that there's an incredible amount of support out there. Find someone who has practical knowledge— knowledge gained from experience. I've known people in real estate who have all these initials after their names and the only thing they don't have is *m.o.n.e.y.* All they have are degrees. They're into "learning," but as Tony Robbins told me, "Alex, don't let your learning lead to knowledge. Let your learning lead to *action*. What's really interesting is this: if you are stupid and broke that's okay; but if you are smart and broke it's a sin!"

The solution is to seek out people who are knowledgeable and take that knowledge and apply it, practice it, role-play it, work with it, and get better at it! And that's what I teach in my trainings.

### Wright

What a great thought and a great conversation. Today we've been talking with Alex Szinegh. He is the Senior Regional VP for North America, Exit Realty Corporation International. And as we have found out today, he tells it like it is from his experience, which is real knowledge.

Thank you so much, Alex, for being with us today on *Speaking of Success*.

### Szinegh

Thank you, David. I'm hoping that when people pick up this book they understand that they can accomplish anything in life if they set their mind to it! They can if they evolve and surround themselves with enough people who can support them and who know what to do.

I'm hoping that people will take this part of the book and dissect it and call me or send me an e-mail. Whether they have a problem or if they are just on the way up (or on the way down)—whatever direction—I want them to let me know what they're thinking.

I made a DVD series, and on the front of that DVD there's a sign that says "No Bull." We say it like it is—I will tell you the truth. Unfortunately, most people don't want to know the truth, but I'll tell you the truth. Please get in touch with us and give us your comments.

# About the Author

ALEX ZOLTAN SZINEGH is Senior Regional VP for North America, Exit Realty Corp International. Alex is a true "rags to riches" story. Armed with only a grade ten education, this immigrant from Hungary has surmounted all odds to become an internationally recognized Speaker, Trainer, and Coach. Alex has personally *sold* over 2,300 properties, he has run successful businesses, and trained thousands of people in the art of "street smarts" and "how to succeed in spite your circumstances and past." Alex is refreshing, funny, educational, and positively "in your face" with has candid style. He tells it like it is. Alex is a family man with four children ages thirty-six, thirty-two, twenty-nine, and a four-year-old. He also has five grandchildren. Alex's main drive to succeed in life has been his family. His biggest supporter and inspiration is wife Cindy.

**Alex Zoltan Szinegh**
P.O Box 750516
Las Vegas, NV 89136-0516
Phone: 702.334.5570
E-mail: alexszinegh@exitrealty.com
www.alexszinegh.com
www.ExitOnlineUniversity.com